MILLER'S Royal MEMORABILIA

MILLER'S

Royal
MEMORABILIA

Eric Knowles

Miller's Royal Memorabilia
Eric Knowles

First published in Great Britain in 1994
by Miller's
an imprint of Reed Consumer Books Limited
Michelin House, 81 Fulham Road
London SW3 6RB
and Auckland, Melbourne, Singapore and Toronto

Series Editor Frances Gertler
Editors Alison Macfarlane, Janet Gleeson
Art Editor Mark Winwood
Art Director Tim Foster
Production Heather O'Connell
Index Hilary Bird
Special Photography Ian Booth

A CIP catalogue record for this book is available from
the British Library

ISBN 1 85732 167 7

Set in A Garamond and Univers Condensed
Origination by Scantrans Pte Ltd, Singapore
Produced by Mandarin Offset
Printed in China

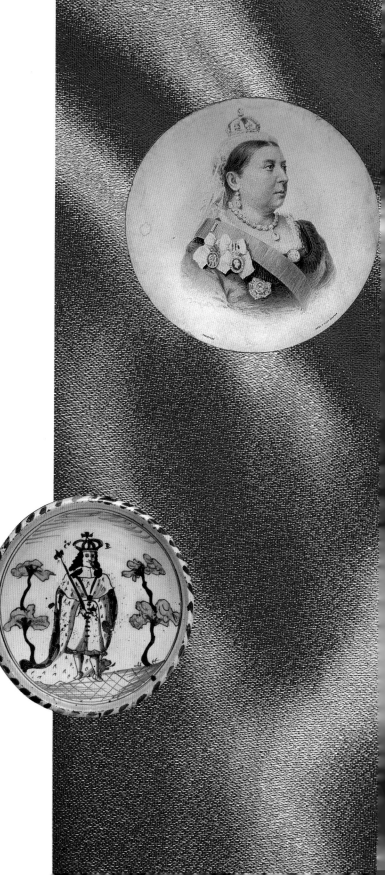

Jacket Illustrations
(Clockwise) Brass corkscrew made for Edward VII's coronation, two
German export figural jugs of George V and Queen Mary made for their
coronation, Corgi toy model of the state coach used for Queen Elizabeth
II at her silver jubilee, a Coventry plate made for Queen Victoria's silver
jubilee, a mug of Prince Charles designed by Mark Boxer

p.2 top: A scalloped plate made for Queen Victoria's silver jubilee; bottom: A plate made in support of George IV's wife, Queen Caroline
p.4 top: A press-card plate made for Queen Victoria's diamond jubilee;
bottom: A London delft blue dash charger of Charles II in his coronation
robes, c.1685
p.5 top: A Prattware jug with a portrait of Admiral Lord Nelson; bottom
left: A large circular plate made by Paragon for the Empire Exhibition in
Scotland, 1933; bottom right: Parian busts of Prince Albert and Princess
Alexandra, made for their wedding, 1863

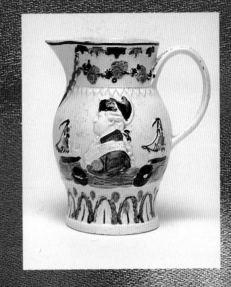

Contents

Introduction

Centuries of pomp and circumstance accorded to royal and patriotic occasions have left a legacy of commemorative memorabilia, the diversity of which continues to surprise even the most seasoned collector. These items provide an attractive and colourful record of important events in history and demonstrate what the buying public have seen as occasions worth remembering. Anyone starting a collection of royal memorabilia will see not only many interesting pieces during their search, but will acquire a comprehensive knowledge of the way their ancestors lived. Included in these pages are items produced for the many political and social events which have also been commemorated over the years with equal enthusiasm to that for royal occasions.

By far the greatest number of royal and political commemoratives are ceramics. Britain has produced generations of potters who have been quick to recognize the commercial possibilites the procession of historical events could afford. Output was further increased by the various aldermen and dignitaries of the towns and cites who delved deep into their own pockets to ensure that countless schoolchildren received a free gift of a mug or beaker in celebration of a royal event, be it coronation, jubilee or marriage. In return, the donators are themselves often accorded lasting recognition on the reverse of the gift. These early "freebies" constitute for many the first seeds of what was later to become a more comprehensive collection of royal memorabilia.

Quality of design and craftsmanship has often suffered at the hand of over-zealous enthusiasm, although some attempts were made to maintain standards by the British Pottery Manufacturers Federation (set up in 1935), which released a series of official designs for royal events which it continues to produce today. In the early years of this century, Thomas Goode & Co introduced the idea of commissioning special limited editions from the major makers of ceramics and these are still issued, with Minton, Spode and Wedgwood all producing special collectors' pieces which command a premium.

Coronations and jubilees have always accorded the greatest public attention, and it is usually those items recording the rarer events which hold the most appeal – for example a mug produced to commemorate Queen Elizabeth II's visit to a small town to open a fete, or a jug showing the amnesty of naval deserters in Liverpool, produced during the reign of George III, are always desirable.

Although ceramics dominate the commemorative market there is a plethora of other items available to the collector with prices to suit every pocket: biscuit tins, horse brasses, printed ephemera, Victorian woven silk pictures, playing cards, jigsaw puzzles, autographs, photographs, and even items as bizarre as Queen Victoria's underwear and a biscuit made for the wedding of Prince Charles and Lady Dina have been offered for sale in recent years. Many collectors specialize in collecting ceramics, but there are many others who wish to collect the more unusual and obscure.

Royal memorabilia has gradually risen in popularity, and an increasing number of items are being produced as people have acquired a greater awareness of political, social and royal events. Consequently there have been far more items produced for the reign of Elizabeth II than ever before; while items from the earliest commemorated reign, of Charles I, are both exceptionally rare and very expensive. Although some regard recent items as less desirable, if only because of their far greater numbers, they are important in giving continuity to any collection and are bound to become cherished items in years to come as many fall foul to breakage or loss. Collectors may wish to build up their collection by monarch or by medium, but no matter how one chooses to collect, the opportunites are endless. Shops specialize in royal memorabilia, all the major auction houses have specialist royal memorabilia sales, and many more bargains can be found at the numerous second hand and antique shops and fairs throughout the country.

This book aims to guide the collector through the plethora of collectables on the market, and point out the variety and quality, giving where possible a price guide. It also aims to place each monarch in a historical and social context so that the collector can relive the past during their treasure quest. I hope this book will pass on some of the enthusiasm I have for the subject and inspire you in your search for new and exciting items– happy hunting!

ERIC KNOWLES

Stuarts and Hanoverians

From James I (1603-1625)

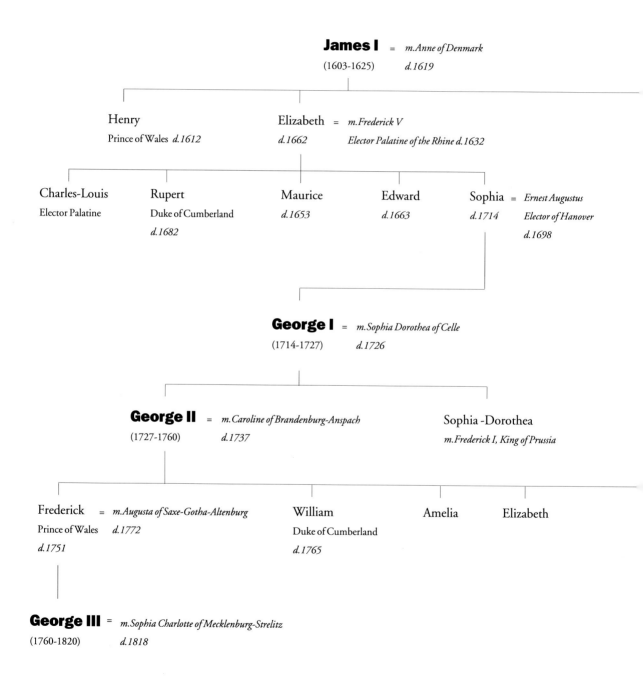

James I = *m.Anne of Denmark*
(1603-1625)   *d.1619*

Henry   Elizabeth   =   *m.Frederick V*
Prince of Wales *d.1612*   *d.1662*   *Elector Palatine of the Rhine d.1632*

Charles-Louis   Rupert   Maurice   Edward   Sophia   =   *Ernest Augustus*
Elector Palatine   Duke of Cumberland   *d.1653*   *d.1663*   *d.1714*   *Elector of Hanover*
                     d.1682   *d.1698*

George I = *m.Sophia Dorothea of Celle*
(1714-1727)   *d.1726*

George II = *m.Caroline of Brandenburg-Anspach*   Sophia -Dorothea
(1727-1760)   *d.1737*   *m.Frederick I, King of Prussia*

Frederick   =   *m.Augusta of Saxe-Gotha-Altenburg*   William   Amelia   Elizabeth
Prince of Wales   *d.1772*   Duke of Cumberland
d.1751   *d.1765*

George III = *m.Sophia Charlotte of Mecklenburg-Strelitz*
(1760-1820)   *d.1818*

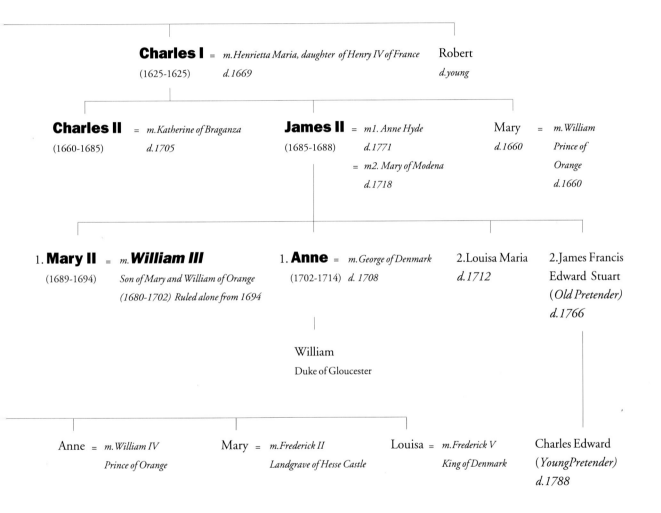

Charles I = *m. Henrietta Maria, daughter of Henry IV of France*   Robert

(1625-1625)   *d. 1669*   *d. young*

Charles II = *m. Katherine of Braganza*   **James II** = *m1. Anne Hyde*   Mary = *m. William*

(1660-1685)   *d. 1705*   (1685-1688)   *d. 1771*   *d. 1660*   *Prince of*

= *m2. Mary of Modena*   *Orange*

d. 1718   *d. 1660*

1. **Mary II** = *m.* **William III**   1. **Anne** = *m. George of Denmark*   2. Louisa Maria   2. James Francis

(1689-1694)   *Son of Mary and William of Orange*   (1702-1714) *d. 1708*   *d. 1712*   Edward Stuart

(1680-1702) Ruled alone from 1694   *(Old Pretender)*

d. 1766

William

Duke of Gloucester

Anne = *m. William IV*   Mary = *m. Frederick II*   Louisa = *m. Frederick V*   Charles Edward

Prince of Orange   *Landgrave of Hesse Castle*   *King of Denmark*   *(Young Pretender)*

d. 1788

From Hanover to Windsor

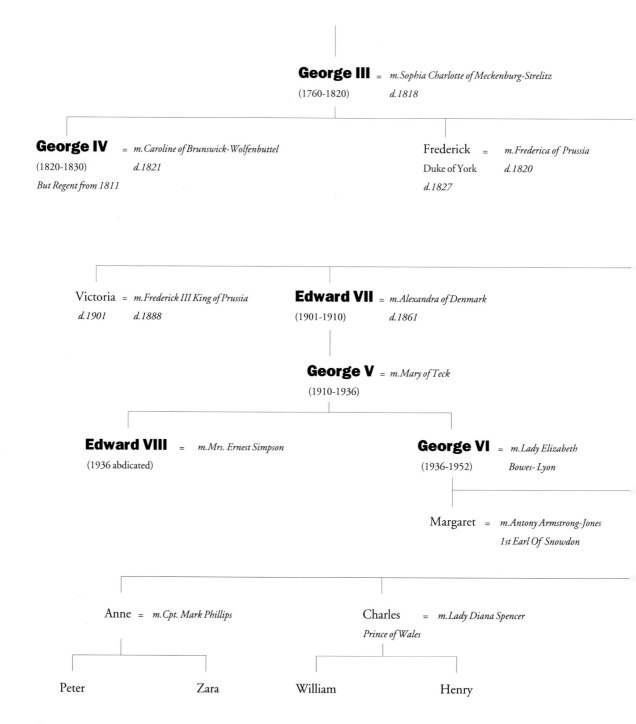

George III = m. Sophia Charlotte of Meckenburg-Strelitz
(1760-1820)   d.1818

George IV = m. Caroline of Brunswick-Wolfenbuttel
(1820-1830)   d.1821
But Regent from 1811

Frederick = m. Frederica of Prussia
Duke of York   d.1820
d.1827

Victoria = m. Frederick III King of Prussia
d.1901   d.1888

Edward VII = m. Alexandra of Denmark
(1901-1910)   d.1861

George V = m. Mary of Teck
(1910-1936)

Edward VIII = m. Mrs. Ernest Simpson
(1936 abdicated)

George VI = m. Lady Elizabeth
(1936-1952)   Bowes- Lyon

Margaret = m. Antony Armstrong-Jones
1st Earl Of Snowdon

Anne = m. Cpt. Mark Phillips

Charles = m. Lady Diana Spencer
Prince of Wales

Peter   Zara

William   Henry

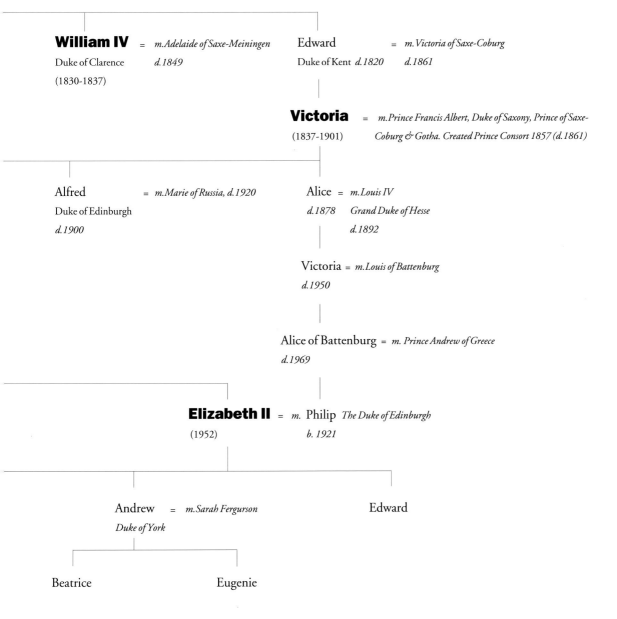

William IV = *m.Adelaide of Saxe-Meiningen*   Edward   = *m.Victoria of Saxe-Coburg*
Duke of Clarence   *d.1849*   Duke of Kent *d.1820*   *d.1861*
(1830-1837)

Victoria = *m.Prince Francis Albert, Duke of Saxony, Prince of Saxe-*
(1837-1901)   *Coburg & Gotha. Created Prince Consort 1857 (d.1861)*

Alfred   = *m.Marie of Russia, d.1920*   Alice = *m.Louis IV*
Duke of Edinburgh   *d.1878*   *Grand Duke of Hesse*
d.1900   *d.1892*

Victoria = *m.Louis of Battenburg*
d.1950

Alice of Battenburg = *m. Prince Andrew of Greece*
d.1969

Elizabeth II = *m.* Philip *The Duke of Edinburgh*
(1952)   *b. 1921*

Andrew = *m.Sarah Fergurson*   Edward
Duke of York

Beatrice   Eugenie

Carolean & Stuart

(1625-1685)

Charles I, the second son of King James I, became King of Britain and Ireland on 27 March 1625. He was a deeply religious man, short in stature, shy, artistic and delicate, with a stammer he never managed to overcome. His unswerving nature and Catholic beliefs led to the Civil War between the Parliamentarians and Royalists in 1642. Although the King enlisted the help of the Irish army, the Parliamentarians (Roundheads) were supported by the Scots, and the Royalists (Cavaliers) were defeated by Oliver Cromwell and his New Model Army in 1645. The King surrendered to the Scots a year later and was handed over to the British Parliament. He escaped to the Isle of Wight in 1647, but his continued plotting against Parliament resulted in the second Civil War in 1648. The King was tried and convicted of treason, and on 30 January 1649 he was beheaded outside the Banqueting Hall of Whitehall, still as strong in his convictions as ever.

After the King's death the country was declared a Commonwealth with Oliver Cromwell as Lord Protector, a Puritan who instituted direct military rule until the monarchy was restored under Charles II in 1660. The new King was the antithesis of his father, replacing the former's Puritanism with his flamboyant love of life, and his arrival was greeted with great enthusiasm, as many were happy to see the end of the restrictive years under Cromwell. However, his actions paved the way for more discontent which was to come to a head under James II, and in his final years he ruled without a Parliament. Two significant events during Charles II's reign were the Great Plague (1665) and the Fire of London (1666), seen by many as God's punishment for the country's sins. His reign also saw a revival in the arts and sciences – Christopher Wren designed many fine churches after the Great Fire, including St Paul's Cathedral, and set up the Royal Society; the scientist Isaac Newton made discoveries in the field of gravity; and theatre curtains were lifted to show the Restoration Comedies of

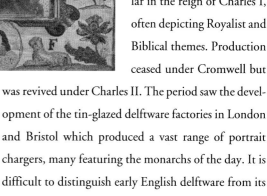

Wycherly and Congreve. Charles II was succeeded in 1685 by his younger brother James II who strongly upheld the beliefs of his father, Charles I. His rule was dominated by his obsessive attempts to promote Catholicism which led British Parliament to call on the King's nephew, William, Prince of Orange, and his wife Mary (James I's daughter by an earlier marriage) to overthrow the King. James II was forced into exile in France in 1688 under the protection of Louis IX, and William and Mary came to the throne.

The 17th century is the earliest period from which commemoratives survive. Ceramics and needlework dominate the market. Stumpwork became popular in the reign of Charles I, often depicting Royalist and Biblical themes. Production ceased under Cromwell but was revived under Charles II. The period saw the development of the tin-glazed delftware factories in London and Bristol which produced a vast range of portrait chargers, many featuring the monarchs of the day. It is difficult to distinguish early English delftware from its Dutch counterparts but any items that feature Charles I and II are likely to be English, as there was little export trade at this time.

Left: A blue dash delft equestrian charger depicting Charles II, c.1670-75, 12⅞in (32.7cm).

Above: A stumpwork and beadwork mirror frame incorporating portraits of Charles II and Queen Catherine, c.1670.

Charles I & II
(1649-85)

Commemorative pieces made during the reign of Charles I were few and far between, although there are some very rare examples of tin–glazed chargers. Stumpwork (raised embroidery) of the period often depicted Charles I and his Queen, the French Princess Henrietta Maria, who was an unpopular choice with the British public. Following the austere Commonwealth period under Cromwell, the Restoration of the monarchy in 1660 and the arrival of Charles II was greeted with a tumultuous welcome, signalling a rapid and surging growth of wares depicting the new King and Queen. It is interesting to note that a number of wares celebrating Charles II were made during the reign of Queen Anne to show support for the Jacobite cause (see also pp. 18-21).

▲ **This English delft plate from 1715 is relatively naive: note the decorative technique of rough sponging in the tree. However, the polychrome decoration makes it attractive. The absence of "II" beside the "C" has resulted in the plate being wrongly ascribed to Charles I. The chips on the rim do not affect the value as tin-glaze chips easily.**

£3,000-4,000

▼ **This polychrome wine cup, used for drinking mulled beverages, is an extremely precious item as tin-glaze is the most expensive collecting area of British pottery. Dated to 1662, it shows a portrait of Charles II. Even though the enamel has flaked, the cup is still worth over £40,000.**

£40,000-44,000

► **Stumpwork grew in popularity during the reign of Charles I and transformed needlework into a 3-dimensional art form. Most subjects tended to be biblical or classical themes. Surviving portraits of Charles I and Queen Henrietta Maria are relatively scarce. This stumpwork picture of the King and Queen is one of the finest that has appeared on the open market. Their attire, facial detail and clothing are of a high standard and well preserved, considering that stumpwork is made of a fragile silk background that deteriorates quite rapidly in comparison with most other fabrics.**

£10,000-15,000

◄ This needlework panel of 1663, worked in coloured silk and metal threads, depicts scenes from the life of Charles II. These include the King's escape to France dressed as the servant of Jane Lane, the sister of one of his colonels. The composition, quality and number of figures all contribute to its value. The details are in raised work, moss work and detached buttonhole stitch embellished with seed pearls.

£10,000

▼ Pill slabs are quite rare. At one time they were believed to have been used by apothecaries for preparing drugs, but they are now thought to have been used as shop window displays. This polychrome example is probably the ultimate piece for a collector. The inscribed initials: NB may refer to Nat Bateman or Nicholas Bannister who were registered apothecaries during this period.

£15,000-20,000

▲ The blue and white colour scheme of English delft was developed out of an attempt to imitate Chinese blue and white porcelain. The influence and popularity of Oriental china is evident in the Chinese border of this tin-glaze earthenware plate. It was made in 1745, long after Charles's reign, to show Jacobite support for the dispossessed King.

£1,000-1,200

▼ This slipware dish by William Talor is exceptionally rare and highly desirable despite the naive artistic representation of Charles II. Alongside Thomas Toft, Taylor was regarded as the foremost potter working during this period.

£30,000

Beware of slipware fakes, which give themselves away by slick and sopisticated decoration and a light weight.

The Jacobites

The Jacobites were supporters of the Stuart line which lost power after the deposition of James II and their sympathies were linked to their religious affiliations with the Catholic church. After James's death the Jacobite cause revolved around his son James Edward and grandson, Charles Edward, the Old and Young Pretenders. In 1715, the Old Pretender, calling himself James III, unsuccessfully attempted to instate himself as the rightful king in the first Jacobite uprising. In 1745, his son, the Young Pretender, led a second, again unsuccessful, attempt to restore the crown to the Stuart line. They conducted their intrigues from the relative safety of France, where James Edward was known as the Chevalier St George and Charles as Bonnie Prince Charlie. Jacobite memorabilia is characterized by the clandestine use of symbols and motifs to denote sympathy with the Stuart cause. The rose appeared flanked by two rose buds, representing the English Crown and the two Pretenders. Other emblems include the dove, which symbolizes the "Prince across the water", and oak leaves which refer to the Boscobel oak tree in Brewood Forest where Charles II sucessfully hid from Cromwell's troops in 1651 during earlier unrest between the Stuart King and the Roundheads. Commemoratives include Jacobite glasses, loving cups inscribed "Success to Bonnie Prince Charlie", and black glazed wares with painted coloured enamel.

▼ Because saltglazed wares could withstand the heat of boiling water they were well-suited to teapots. This example is moulded with shells and oak leaves, and is painted with a portrait of Bonnie Prince Charlie as a Highlander. The "Pectin-shell" decoration was often applied to silver pieces of the period. The red roses represent the two Pretenders.

£2,000-3,000

▲ This cylindrical Jacobite tankard from c.1745 was made by the Jackfield pottery in Staffordshire which specialized in wares with a red earthenware body covered in a black glaze and enamelled, and frequently bearing slogans promoting the Jacobite cause. Black glazed wares, particularly with floral decoration, were also made in Staffordshire and these are often erroneously called Jackfield, as is a great deal of later, Victorian black glaze. This tankard bears the hopeful slogan "God Save the King" in reference to Bonnie Prince Charlie.

£1,000-5,000

▼ Prince James Edward Stuart was the focal point of the Jacobite cause during the 1715 rebellion which proved a disaster for his supporters. He made an untimely arrival on Scottish soil after the rebellion had faltered and two Scottish lords – Earl Derwentwater and Viscount Kenmure – were beheaded for supporting the cause. Painted portrait miniatures became popular in the 16th century and continued to

▲ This saltglazed stoneware mug from c.1745-50 is beautifully made and enamelled using the adventurous palette typical of the period. The white rose is a recurring Jacobite symbol. The Scotsman, in a comic stance, is wielding a claymore.

£1,500-2,000

flourish until the introduction of the daguerreotype (one of the earliest forms of photography) in the mid-19th century. This portrait mounted in a silver frame depicts the youthful Prince wearing armour and an Order of the Garter sash.

£1,500-2,500

▶ Items were also produced in support of the Hanovarian cause. This mug was made in China for export and the Chinese influence is clear in the flowers and the portrait of the Duke of Cumberland who has a distinctly Oriental air. The Duke led his troops to victory at Culloden, scene of the last great Jacobite land battle on British soil in 1746.

£1,500-2,000

BONNIE PRINCE CHARLIE

was an ill-educated but charming and handsome man. He came to England against the advice of both his father and Louis XIV of France and many of the people in his army were forced with threats of violence to join the Jacobite cause. He ended his years as an ageing debauchee in Italy and was reputed to be a wife beater. In a memorial in St Peter's in Rome to him and his brother Henry, Cardinal of York, the prince looks young and girlish, which has gained him the title "bonnie".

▼ This silver dog collar with a Jacobite inscription highlights the wide variety of commemoratives that can be found from this period. The inside of this piece is inscribed "Collar of an Italian Greyhound presented to Lady Threepland (*sic*) by Prince Charles Edward Stuart, year 1750".

£1,500-2,000

▼ Spoons were laid on their backs so the inscriptions supporting the Jacobites would be hidden. "Moyses Britannicus" refers to the Old Pretender, who was seen as the liberator of the Scots in the same way that Moses was of the Israelites.

£300-500 the set

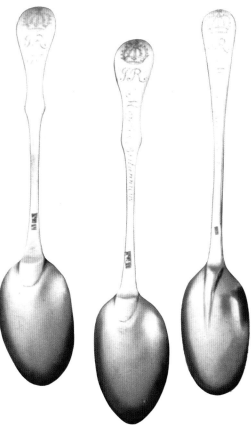

▲ Of all Jacobite artefacts, rings are the most personal. Most were inscribed with patriotic words; two here read "Awa Whigs Awa" (the Whig Party was recognized by the Jacobites as their main adversary at Westminster); others make plaintive appeals for a change of heart and political allegiance, such as the one that reads "Do come".

£100-300 each

▼ During this clandestine period many boxes concealed forbidden subjects, which were often erotic. This heart-shaped snuff box in petrified wood is set with an oval hardstone cameo depicting a dog and is seemingly innocent. However, its contents are of a forbidden political nature – inside is a painted portrait miniature of Bonnie Prince Charlie.

£4,000-6,000

▼ Colour portraits on glass are highly sought-after. This glass from c.1765 is one of a set of enamelled portrait wine glasses of which only eight examples are known. The portrait of the Young Pretender is after a miniature by Sir Robert Strange who is thought to have captured Prince Charles's likeness whilst travelling with him during the revolt of 1745; Strange was later pardoned by George III even though he had fought at Culloden, and was knighted for his royal portrait commissions. **£15,000**

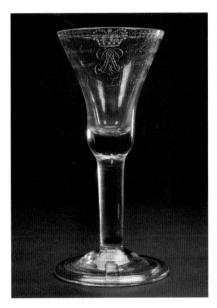

▶ The tradition of enclosing locks of hair in jewelry as mementos was popular for centuries and continued well into the Victorian era. This gold oval pendant locket is surmounted by a coronet and framed by a pierced border. An inscription on the reverse reads "Lock of Prince Charles Edward Stuart's hair 1763". **£300-400**

▲ Amen glasses are so rare and important that each one has a name. This example, entitled the *Gregson of Tilliefour Old Pretender*, is made even more desirable and rare by its shape – out of the 40 Amen glasses known to exist only three have bell-shaped bowls, all the rest are trumpet-shaped. This item is the ultimate piece for any collector of Jacobite glass.

£30,00-40,000

JACOBITE GLASS

Jacobite glasses were used at the secret societies held by supporters of James II and were manufactured up until the Old Pretender's death in 1766. They are engraved with a variety of Stuart mottos and emblems; the rose was particularly popular. Often portraits, such as that of the Young Pretender, featured on glasses; at other times glasses with the word "*Fiat*" ("Let it be done") would appear, originally made for a Cycle Club founded in 1710 by Sir Watkin Williams-Wynn, but beoming a popular slogan on Jacobite wares. Very rare are Amen glasses, engraved with emblems and hymn verses ending with "Amen". Rarest of all are those with coloured enamels, where the enamelling may be very obscure and indistinct, especially around the rim. Jacobite glasses can be identified by their decoration which was usually wheel engraved rather than diamond point etched. As Jacobite glass is highly sought-after many copies exist and although some are very deceptive they tend to be made of flawless glass which appears too perfect to be genuine.

William and Mary & Queen Anne

(1688 -1714)

The arrival in England of William and Mary saw the re-establishment of a Protestant king and allayed fears amongst the clergy of a return to a Catholic monarchy. William's landing at Torbay from Holland on 15 November 1688 was seen as the start of the "Glorious Revolution" and was greeted with unopposed optimism. Within a short period he had suppressed the Irish Catholics and was victorious at the Battle of the Boyne (July 1690). William accepted the throne jointly with his wife and started a period of constitutional monarchy whereby Parliament had to be consulted in matters of the country. Their reign was relatively trouble-free, although William did take his troops to Scotland to quell the Jacobites – supporters of James II who wanted to reinstate who they saw as the deposed King's rightful heir to the throne (see pp. 18-19). William also managed to reconcile Holland and Britain after earlier disharmony, and the two countries now fought together in the War of the Spanish Succession to prevent Louis IV's grandson acquiring the Spanish throne. The fighting lasted 13 years, but unfortunately William did not live to see Britain's victory as he died in 1702.

Mary had died in 1694 and William ruled on his own for his final years. After his death the crown was passed on to Mary's younger sister, Anne. She was married to George, Prince of Denmark who did not play an influential role in the monarchy; and the Queen herself left most of the country's government to her Tory Parliament. In 1707 the Act of Union with Scotland was passed which put an end to a separate Scottish Parliament and gave the country representatives in the House of Commons and House of Lords, allaying fears of the Scots electing their own monarch and giving them an active role in running the now "British" economy. The War of Spanish

Succession was also concluded (1713). More and more countries fell under British rule and the seeds were sown for the great British Empire of Victoria's reign.

Hand-made, hand-painted chargers were the most popular commemoratives of this period and as William and Mary ruled jointly, most feature their portraits together. Examples exist of just William, often on horseback and wearing his crown and robes, but those of Mary alone are very rare and collectable. Decoration consisted mainly of naively-drawn half-portraits, in basic colours of blue and white or in a polychrome palette of blue, yellow, green and manganese. Most were made in Britain, but some with William's portrait were made in Holland before his accession – those made after usually have "W3" above the portrait. On items for Anne's reign, the portrait of her husband never appears on chargers with her picture, but examples do exist bearing his portrait alone, where it is accompanied by the initials "PG" for Prince George. Although the commemorative market was dominated by pottery, stumpwork continued to be produced; and a number of pressed horn items were also made, particularly in the form of snuff boxes made by Obrissett.

Left: A silver-mounted tortoisehell snuff box c.1710 depicting Queen Anne, 2⁷/₈in (7.3cm) long.

Above: A very rare Staffordshire slipware portrait charger of Prince William and Queen Mary, by Thomas Sanford, c.1690.

William & Mary
(1689-1702)

The Dutch Prince William accepted the crown of Britain on condition that his wife Mary share the throne with him. The reign of William and Mary is marked by the strong Dutch influence in the decorative arts, especially with the introduction of marquetry, walnut furniture and tin-glaze wares. The King and Queen proved popular subjects and were commemorated in portrait plates, stumpwork and glasses. Blue dash chargers are generally the most sought-after commemoratives of their reign and they remained fashionable until the George I period, using the same colours and naively drawn designs, and usually featuring the initials of the monarch which helps with identification. William and Mary are often attired in ermine robes and sceptres. Pieces bearing equestrian portraits are always very desirable and they increase in value when initialled and dated. Tin-glaze chargers easily fetch over £8,000, even with the inevitable chips and cracks on the rims.

▼ This delft blue dash charger of c.1690 is attractively decorated in a typical design of polychrome with blue sponged trees and yellow lines. Although of a type also made in Bristol, Brislington and Delft, the potting characteristics of this charger suggest it is a London piece. Difficulties of attribution abound and experts still disagree over the distinguishing features of London and Bristol pieces.

£17,000

▲ Delft chargers made in Holland have very clear stylistic differences to those made in Britain. They are sometimes heavier and have distinctive borders; this example has an elaborate border specific to Dutch factories. Dutch pieces also have a slightly pink tinge to the glaze, especially noticeable on the reverse. Locating where a piece was made can be difficult as many Dutch craftsmen migrated to Britain during the period. This needs to be taken into account, as Dutch delft tends to be less desirable than English delft.

£800-1,000

▼ Monochrome plates tend to be less desirable than their polychrome counterparts. This London delft Royal Portrait plate of c.1689 is a quirky representation of King William and Queen Mary, who are depicted in an amusing and comical half-length portrait.

£1,500

▶ Size affects the value of a piece. Athough this Brislington charger lacks the sophistication of the earlier similar example featured above, it commands a greater price because it is of larger proportions.

£4,000-6,000

▲ This Dutch delft dish shows an unusually risqué portrait of the Queen with a bare breast. An orange pigment had not yet been perfected and William of Orange had to be satisfied with a strong yellow! This plate of c.1690 follows the typical Dutch lobed form and may reflect an influence of earlier metalwork forms.

£1,500-2,000 a pair

▼ The slipware technique was popularized by Thomas Toft and William Talor. This dish, attributed to Ralph Simpson, portrays a wide-eyed king in what could almost be called a caricature, with regalia of sword, sceptre and sash of

office. Rather surprisingly, William's left hand is twisted in a loop, as if his arm were made of elastic! The lattice border of dark and light is typical of slipware. Such examples are extremely rare and despite their damaged condition still fetch a high price.

£30,000 -40,000

▼ This Brislington delft Royal portrait charger is an unusual item as not many examples survive showing Queen Mary on her own – it may have been one of a pair with another portraying King William. It is decorated in the typical palette of polychrome blue, white, yellow and manganese (a purple-like colour). Queen Mary is wearing a yellow necklace of pearls (her usual decoration) and has a manganese and yellow crown perched delicately on top of her head.

£2,000-3,000

Queen Anne
(1702-14)

Among the most significant and commemorated events of Anne's reign were the Act of Union with Scotland in 1707 and the Battle of Blenheim during the war of the Spanish Succession. The rose and thistle are often entwined on pottery to celebrate the Act of Union, and a number of equestrian chargers were produced to celebrate the victor of Blenheim, the Duke of Marlborough. Queen Anne's husband, Prince George of Denmark, also appears on pottery but because artistic representations of the human form tend not to be realistic, it is sometimes difficult to distinguish between portraits of the consort and the Duke of Marlborough. Other commemorative items from this time include needlework pictures, stumpwork and pressed horn snuff boxes. However, the majority of extant pieces tend to be blue dash chargers.

▲ An increasing sophistication in decorative techniques on royal portrait chargers can be seen in this example from c.1705. There is much greater detail in the branches of the green sponged trees and also in the blue dashes of the sky than on earlier examples made during the reigns of King Charles I and II (see pp. 16-17). Individual touches such as the jaunty angle of the Queen's crown make this a lively and sought-after piece. The style of the lettering suggests that the charger was made at either the Bristol or Brislington potteries.

£10,000-15,000

▼ The addition of yellow to this predominantly blue delft Bristol charger will increase its desirability. The painted portrait of Queen Anne shows her seated in her Coronation robes Interestingly, the Queen is nearly always shown with a plunging neckline! Blue dash chargers, although the most prevalent type of commemorative of this period, are still very rare and valuable. This charger is

relatively large (13 ¼in, 33.5cm diameter), and this will increase its value, despite the fact that the dashes on the border have degenerated into dots.

£10,000-15,000

▶ Act of Union plates fetch considerably less than portrait plates even though they are very rare. The painted decoration of the English rose and Scottish thistle is typical.

£2,000-3,000

▼ Prince George of Denmark is shown here in military guise holding a baton, the symbol of a military commander.

There are very similar portrait plates of the Duke of Marlborough — the initials are often the only way to identify the subject, and they also add to the value.

£6,000-8,000

► Grinling Gibbons was one of the greatest wood carvers to have worked in England. Consequently, this large carved limewood coronation relief of Queen Anne, c.1702, from his workshops is extremely desirable. The Queen is portrayed in profile beneath the crown of England, wearing the Garter Star, and surrounded by a rich relief of fruit, flowers and vegetables, which are characteristic of Gibbons' work.

£10,00-12,000

▼ Crooked compositions are not unusual for delftware as it was all handmade. In fact, it adds to their charm and individuality. This plate of c.1702 shows the Queen standing flanked by the usual decorative motif of blue sponged trees and again dressed in coronation robes.

£2,000-3,000

▲ This plate has the same composition as the one above left, but shows the Duke of Marlborough who was general of the army in 1711. Even though the colours of this plate are more vibrant than on the one portraying Prince George, it is priced lower: usually the more famous the subject, the more desirable the object. However, a dated plate of a general may be worth more than an undated royal portrait charger.

£4,000-6,000

George I & II
(1714 - 1760)

Anne died without an heir and the British Parliament, looking for a Protestant descendant of the Stuart line, offered the crown to George the Elector of Hanover, the great-grandson of James I. When he came to the throne in 1714 he couldn't speak a word of English and generally disliked Britain, returning to Hanover as often as he could. In 1715 he quelled the Jacobite uprising led by the Old Pretender, James Francis Edward, son of James II, who believed he was the rightful heir to the British throne (see pp.18-21). George inherited a Whig government led by Robert Walpole, whose many achievements included restoring confidence in the government after the "South Sea Bubble" affair in 1720 when stocks set up to trade with South America crashed disastrously. However, it was generally an uneventful time and a period of dynastic stability, with the King resurrecting the Stuart line and securing a strong position in the world for Britain.

When George I died in 1727 George II succeeded his father to the throne in the first conventional succession of a monarch in Britain since James II in 1685. Setting a trend that was to continue with a succession of kings, father and son disliked each other intensely; the Prince had been expelled from the palace in 1717 and was only frostily reconciled with his father three years later with the help of Walpole. During George II's reign a second Jacobite rebellion was staged (in 1745), led by King James II's grandson, the Young Pretender, and in the last land battle fought in Britain the Jacobites were defeated at Culloden in 1746 by an army skilfully managed by the King's son, the Duke of Cumberland. George II's reign saw Britain's glory in the Seven Years' War against France, although peace was not settled until 1763. The British Empire was also taking hold – a series of victories over France put Canada, Guadaloupe and Senegal under British control. By the time of the King's death the Hanovarians had gained in popularity, and it was for George II that the first British national anthem was sung, at a gala theatre performance.

Britain's increasing stronghold on the world opened the doors for improved trade abroad. Manufacturers began to order porcelain from China decorated with British designs. These import pieces were particularly fashionable with wealthy families who ordered entire dinner services decorated with their family crests. It is interesting to note that sometimes the Chinese took the instructions so literally that some items exist where the instruction itself has been incorporated into the decoration. Many commemoratives support the Hanovarian cause against the Jacobites, showing loyalty to the King, but pieces were also made in support of the Jacobites. Somewhat incongruously, some glass made during George II's reign, known as Williamite glass, commemorates the earlier King, William III, as he was seen as the original defender of the Protestant cause. Delftware was beginning to wane in popularity by the 1750s because of the import of Chinese porcelain and the emergeance of porcelain manufacturers in Britain, in Chelsea, Bow, Derby, Bristol and Worcester. Hand-painted decoration still dominated on pottery and ceramics, as transfer printing designs onto wares was developed only in the last year of George II's reign.

Left: A portrait of Prince James Francis Edward (the Old Pretender) by Cosmo Alexander, 1749.

Above: A rare Williamite colour-twist wine glass from the late 18th century, ht 5¾in (14.5cm).

George I
(1714-1727)

Chargers were the commonest commemoratives during the reign of George I. Decoration became more elaborate and adventurously designed with foliate borders. The quality of painting began to improve and was more refined, and new colours of green, iron red and cobalt blue were introduced. The chief centres of production were Lambeth and Southwark. It can be difficult to identify the origins of a piece, as Bristol was still active, as was Lambeth, and all used a similar colour glaze – pieces from Brislington tend to have more elaborate borders.

▲ The border of this George II portrait charger is very detailed and shows great sophistication in stylistic techniques. However, a highly elaborate border does not necessarily mean a higher price – it is likely that a plate with a simpler border which is initialled and dated will command a higher figure.

£4,000-6,000

◀ Equestrian figures are sought after because they convey a sense of the active and dramatic which is evident in this crowned figure of George I, shown in profile astride a stallion. This is a very rare Staffordshire press-moulded slipware dish and is attributed to Samuel Malkin, a renowned craftsman of the time. Its large size — 13 1/4 in (34 cm) – and its scarcity increase its value and desirability.

£35,000-50,000

▲ In the absence of a portrait, royal or otherwise, patriotic verses will add to the value of a plate, as will the inclusion of the date, as on this plate which is one of a series of year plates. A favoured decorative motif of the time was the green garland, a symbol of the victorious, and on this example it encloses the inscription "God Save King George 1716".

£2,000

▼ The use of more adventurous colours than in earlier years is evident in this Lambeth delft charger. The border is also elaborate, with an orange lattice, stylized foliage and floral patterns. The depiction of the King, although still very static, is a more serious attempt at portraiture of the monarch.

£4,000-6,000

◄ This plate can be traced to Britain rather than Holland by its border, which is characteristic of British delfware. The remarkably intricate initials "KG" adds to its desirability and were obviously worked by a skilled hand. The small size of the plate of 8 3/4 in (22cm) and its lack of variety in colour will give it a lower value.

£2,000-3,000

▼ The lack of initials and the characteristic naivety of the painting on this Bristol royal portrait charger make it difficult to ascertain whether the portrait depicts George I or George II. Very similar examples exist with the initials GI and GII. However, the charger is still highly collectable as the composition is ambitious – the artist has attempted to give character to the monarch's features and has dressed him in a fetching pair of green breeches! The finely painted border and the overall high quality of the charger will also increase its value to collectors.

£8,000-10,000

▲ The subject of Adam and Eve on this diamond-engraved royalist goblet of 1716 suggests it was produced as a marriage goblet. The combination of Adam and Eve with a royalist theme (the glass is inscribed "God Save King George") is otherwise unknown and therefore makes this piece highly collectable. The value of the glass is further enhanced by the fact that it is one of the earliest examples of pedestal stem glasses in England. The painting of Adam and Eve can also be found on contemporary English delftware, particularly on that produced in Bristol.

£25,000-35,000

George II
(1727-60)

George II became King upon the death of his father George I in 1727 and reigned for 33 years. Although King for far longer than his father, there are surprisingly fewer commemoratives for him, particularly in delftware. One of the most significant events of George II's reign was the second Jacobite uprising of 1745 which spawned a host of wares, particularly focussing on the activities of the Duke of Cumberland, and the defeat of the Jacobites. George II is important in the history of royal commemoratives, as he was the first King to have his portrait printed on ceramics when the technique of transfer printing onto paper was developed at Worcester.

▼ This Bristol blue dash portrait charger celebrating George II's coronation is colourfully enamelled. The initials help with dating as there is little to tell this example from those of Charles II's reign – potters continued with the same formula through the reign of both Georges. Regional variations exist in the decoration – for example, the trees may differ.

▲ Ceramics gradually began to move towards more expensive and delicate pieces, evident in the high-quality transfer printing on this fine white porcelain mug. The portrait of the King is after the artist Thomas Worlidge. The mug, known as First Period Worcester, was made when Dr John Wall was a partner at the factory in Worcester where this piece was made. If perfect, its value would be around £1,500 but because of a crack in its base, the price falls.

£6,000-8,000

£800-1,200

▲ As there is very little pottery depicting George II's wife Caroline Ansbach, whom he married in 1705, and even less commemorating her death in 1737, this plate in remembrance of her is both very rare and important. Painted in funereal manganese, the simple, clear cut design and geometric borders add to the sombre tone of the subject.

£2,000-3,000

▶ The Duke of Cumberland finally defeated the Jacobite attempts to overthrow George II when he led his troops to battle at Culloden in 1746. He forced Charles Edward Stuart to flee to France, and through his bloodthirsty actions earnt himself the nickname of "Butcher" Cumberland (see also pp. 18-19). Following the defeat of the Jacobites, Protestant fervour and patriotic feeling ran high during the reign of George II. These sentiments are commemorated in this glass tankard from the time of the battle, which proclaims "God Blefs (sic) King George the Second". The decorative oval cartouche, engraved with an equestrian figure on a prancing horse, is executed in a sophisticated manner.

£1,000-1,500

▼ This Staffordshire teapot is based on the unglazed Yi-Hsing red stoneware winepots exported with tea from the Kuantung Province to Britain in the 17th century. It is similar to the "Astbury wares" of John Astbury and Son who made glazed redwares with applied relief in white clay – the spout and handle have both been applied in this way. This piece is quite rare and its value is increased by the appliquéd royal arms; without them it would be worth only 1/4 of its value.

£2,000-3,000

George III
(1760 - 1820)

George II's young grandson came to the throne in 1760 as the King's son, Frederick, had died in 1751. George III's reign was marked by political and social instability. The young King was impressionable and, ill-advised by his domineering mother and his chief minister, the Earl of Bute, he tried to govern the country through "The King's Friends", his own party made up of the Court and Treasury. The King ousted the Whig oligarchy led by William Pitt and appointed a succession of his own ministers, which lost him considerable support. It was not until the latter years of his reign that the country was ruled by a government supported by both King and Parliament, when William Pitt the Younger was elected Prime Minister in 1784. Although a period of greater stability, changes in political policy and the King's increasing ill-health led to a gradual diminishing of power of the monarchy. Before his death the King, who lapsed into frequent periods of madness, established the Regency Act in 1811 which secured his son as Prince Regent and next in line to the throne. George III's reign was a time of social upheaval; 1780 saw the worst riots in English history between the Catholics and the Papists; and in the early years of the Industrial Revolution in 1811 vast groups of workers, known as Luddites, organized riots throughout the country and burnt down the new textile machines. It was also a period of conflict abroad. The Seven Years' War was won in 1763 and Britain gained hold of a large part of the world from Canada, the West Indies, India and Africa, to Europe; and in 1781 the American War of Independence was fought and Britain was forced to give self rule to the United States. Britain also fought and won two wars with France – the War of Revolution and the Napoleonic Wars which made Lord Nelson a hero.

George III's reign lasted what was then a record 60 years and he is the most commemorated king of the 18th century. Wares appear for his coronation and marriage (in the same year), his jubilee, and his mad-ness and death. The wars spawned a host of patriotic wares, often featuring the British heroes of the day such as the Admirals Vincent, Duncan and Nelson. Always keen to seize any opportunity to produce commemoratives, the British potters also made wares to be exported, probably clandestinely, to the United States to mark the War of Independence; these are usually printed with the portraits of Franklin, Washington and Jefferson. Most items were pottery or porcelain; delftware and redware were now made only in very small quantities, and many of the earlier potteries in Britain had closed down – Chelsea, Bow, Kensington Gore, Bristol and Caughley had disappeared. Creamware, developed by Wedgwood in the early 18th century, grew in popularity. Relatively inexpensive to produce, it soon became the staple for commemoratives, made even more affordable by the development of transfer printing. Relief-moulded jugs were popular; Staffordshire figures were beginning to appear; and prattware was made all over the country. Shapes were changing away from the elaborate Rococo styles of the 1750s to more austere and utilitarian forms, before becoming more flamboyant again during the reign of George IV.

Left: A rare Scottish moulded pottery oval plaque of King George III, 9in (23cm) high.

Above: A Doulton stoneware jug of Nelson, c.1820.

The Coronation
(1761)

George III became King following the sudden death of his grandfather, George II, on 25 October 1760. Although in love with Lady Sarah Lennox, he was forced by his mother into a "proper" marriage with Sophia Charlotte, the youngest daughter of the Duke of Mecklenburg-Strelitz. Two weeks later, in September 1761, George and his Queen were crowned. These events coincided with the introduction of transfer printing on porcelain, and as a result there is a comparatively large number of ceramics made with the King and Queen's effigies and it not always clear which pieces were made specially for the coronation and which were made to celebrate the marriage. Small teapots were popular, as were mugs, portrait medallions and delft plates.

▼ Typical of redware, the decoration on this small teapot and cover is applied. The appliqué figures repre-

sent putti crowning the newly married King and Queen. The shaped footrim is of novel design. Because redware is non-porous, it was seldom glazed.

£1,000-1,500

▼ This London delft plate marks probably one of the last appearances of a British monarch on a painted tin-glaze plate of this type – on later examples printed decoration became the norm. The portrait is far more sophisticated than those of earlier kings and reflects developments in decorative techniques. This example is very rare – it is one of only three

examples ever found. However, its relatively small size of 9in (23cm) diameter will reduce its value. The size and glaze of the plate suggest it was made to commemorate the King's coronation in 1761.

£4,000-6,000

▶ Portraits of both George III and Queen Charlotte are unusual to find together on one item of porcelain, so this rare bell-shaped Worcester mug commands a high price. The portrait of the King was taken from an engraving by Robert Hancock after an original drawing by Jeremiah Meyer. This example can be identified as Worcester by the shape and glaze and by the footrim, which is particular to Worcester factories. However, some other potteries and porcelain manufacturers did use similar techniques.

£3,000-4,000

▼ Although the Worcester factory had a good range of colours, the blue and white decoration which they have used on this First Period cylindrcial mug was much less costly than colour printing, and follows a tradition of emulating earlier Chinese blue and white wares. The single profile portrait of George III is after

an original by Jeremiah Meyer (see also the portrait on the mug on the left); here the King is flanked by a representation of Fame and an early rendition of Britannia. This item is not as rare as some later Worcester wares and bears no marks.

£2,000-3,000

▲ This rare Wedgwood creamware teapot was printed by John Sadler from Liverpool, under an agreement whereby Josiah Wedgwood shipped large quantities of his creamware to Liverpool to be blackprinted, thus greatly reducing the cost of production. The portraits by Thomas Billinge are after originals by Jeremiah Meyer (King George) and Thomas Frye (Queen Charlotte). The prints were originally produced in c.1760 but pottery examples exist bearing the print with the addition of a map of Cuba to celebrate Britain's acquisition of the island in 1762.

£3,000-4,000

▼ Queen Charlotte was one of many leading figures to be depicted in Wedgwood's portrait medallions. This pale blue and white jasperware medallion uses undercutting – a technique not featured on later reproductions, in which the clay is cut manually which results in a better-defined image. The

image on this example would have been taken from a contemporary print.

£500-800

WEDGWOOD

Josiah Wedgwood, who belonged to the fourth generation of a family of potters, revolutionized the pottery industry in Britain. He went into partnership with Thomas Whieldon in Staffordshire in 1754 and spent his early career trying to improve the earthenware body employed at the factory. He established his own business in 1758 and in 1763 developed his famous creamy white earthenware which he covered with a cream-coloured transparent glaze. In 1765 Queen Charlotte comissioned the firm to produce a dinner service with this glaze and Wedgwood renamed the range "Queen's Ware" in her honour. Decoration tended to be transfer-printed (often by Sadler & Green of Liverpool) or enamelled. The new pottery proved such a fine substitute for tin-enamelled pottery that the latter soon ceased production and creamware became the staple earthenware body in the 18th century. Wedgwood also developed a black stoneware called basalt, some famous jasperware and "Etruscan" vases, and introduced a number of revolutionary methods of manufacture .

The American Wars and Social Unrest in Britain

George III's reign was a period of unrest both at home and abroad. In Britain, the Industrial Revolution spawned a host of uprisings, including the Gordon Riots of 1780. Abroad, the Seven Years War (1756-63) was fought between France and England for overseas control, and between the house of Austria and the Kingdom of Prussia for power in Germany. It ended in the Peace Treaty of Paris (1763) between England, France and Spain, and the Treaty of Hubertsberg, which confirmed Prussia as a superpower. The American War of Independence 13 years later (1776-83) was the result of the rising indignation of the British colonies to the control the British Crown had over them. The Americans staged a revolt, helped by the French who joined them in 1778 and the Spanish, who got involved a year later, and although Britain gained many victories, they were forced to surrender at Yorktown. On 4 July 1782 the Declaration of Independence was signed and America became the United States of America.

▲ Lord George Gordon (1751-93) instigated the Gordon Riots in June 1780 in an attempt to repeal the Catholic Reform Act. Many were killed and injured, over 20 rioters were executed and Gordon was tried for high treason. His acquittal is commemorated in this glass portrait medallion by James Tassie, the foremost exponent of these medallions.

£1,850

◄ The outstanding achievements during the Seven Years' War of George III's Commander-in-Chief, Lord Granby, are commemorated in this rare and outstanding English delftware punch-bowl from 1760 which praises him as "Granby the Brave".

£1,500

▼ General James Wolfe (1727-59) played a major role in the Seven Years' War and led the British forces against the French for possession of Quebec in 1759. He managed to capture the strong position but lost his life in the process – on the Heights of Abraham at the age of 32. Wedgwood produced a number of commemoratives to

mark the event, including this jug. The black transfer-printed decoration, depicting the moment of Wolfe's death, is taken from a famous Benjamin West painting which was painted years after Wolfe's death, and it rarely appears on commemorative ceramics.

£1,500

▼ A number of light-hearted pieces were made during this period of political and social unrest in Britain. This creamware tankard was made in Staffordshire c.1790. It is printed with the inscription, "Lord George Riot made a Jew", and bears a humorous print of Lord Gordon about to be circumcized as part of his conversion to Judaism, when his name was changed to Israel Abraham George Gordon.

£1,000-1,500

▲▼ One of the greatest British victories in the American War of Independence was at the Battle of Les Saintes in the West Indies on 12 April 1782, when the French were defeated and command of the Caribbean and the Atlantic was returned to Britain. This very rare Leeds bowl with appliqué decoration shows the French flagship the *Ville de Paris* which was taken during the battle, and the leaders of the British troops, Admiral Lord Hood and Lord General Elliot, Governor of Gibraltar.

£600-800

▲ Warren Hastings was appointed as the first Governor General of India in 1774 but he resigned in 1784 because of increasing conflicts and dishonesty both in India and Britain. On his return to England he was impeached for high crimes and misdemeanours in India, including extortion, and although the trial started in 1788 he was not acquitted until 1795. This paper fan is decorated with a scene of the trial that was printed in 1788. It supports Hastings and reflects his popularity with the public. It is a very rare and serious collectors' item, and the value is enhanced by the decoration on the sticks and end guards at the base of the fan.

£1,250

The French War
(1793-1802)

The French Revolution and the ensuing unrest in which Louis XVI and his Queen were beheaded, led to the French Revolutionary wars, and on 1 February 1793 France declared war on Britain. After early victories at Valenciennes and Brest the war did not go well for the British and it was not until 1797 that they saw any further success when, on February 14, Sir John Jervis, assisted by Nelson, led the British Fleet to victory at the Battle of St Vincent – an achievement which saw Nelson promoted to Rear Admiral and Jervis to Earl St Vincent. The next victory was at Camperdown in October 1797 when Admiral Duncan blockaded the Dutch fleet in the mouth of the River Texel. Two of the three Dutch fleets were destroyed and their flagship and Admiral were captured. In 1798 Nelson took his fleet to Egypt to follow the French; at Aboukir bay he blew up their flagship *L'Orient* and destroyed all but two of their ships, earning himself the title Hero of the Nile. Hostilities came to a close in 1801-2 when the Peace of Amiens was signed, although war quickly resumed in 1803 (see pp. 44-5).

▲ Pearlware, a finer form of creamware with a bluish tinge to the body, was developed by Josiah Wedgwood in the 1770s, and was used by many Staffordshire potters in the late 18th century. This example bears the recurring subject of the Duke of York assembled with his troops at Valenciennes. Here, coloured enamels have been applied to the black transfer printed design; other examples are in two colours.

£500-700

◄ This black-printed jug features a striking equestrian portrait of Frederick, Duke of York, the Commander-in-chief of the British army, as he rallies his troops to battle at Valenciennes where they achieved one of their early victories. This battle was followed by Earl Howe's defeat of the French fleet at Brest in 1794 under the commandership of Admiral Joyeuese, where seven French ships were destroyed. This mug bears the printers' details, which state that it was printed in Liverpool.

£800-900

▼ There was intense interest in the new invention by M. Guillotine used to behead Louis XVI in 1793. This Staffordshire pearlware mug has a macabre illustration of the beheading machine. The design has been transfer printed in blue, but examples also exist in black. The

cream body of the mug has a crackled glaze.

£600-900

▲ This West Country slipware storage jar is a fine example of the rustic pottery made in the late 18th century. It was made to celebrate the British pride in Nelson's victories. "God Save the King" on the reverse reflects patriotic fervour at this time.

£1,000-1,200

▲ This pearlware jug was made in Staffordshire to commemorate the outbreak of war with France in 1793. The body has been decorated with underglaze blue printed decoration. On one side is the royal coat of arms, and on the other a patriotic verse which reads "May Briton true/Their rights pursue/And ever espouse the cause/of Church and King/And every thing/That constitutes their laws". The relative scarcity of pearlware makes this example highly collectable today.

£1,000-1,500

▼ This prattware jug, moulded in low relief, portrays the figure of the Duke of York on a prancing horse. A similar jug exists with portraits of the Duke and the Prince of Coburg, commander-in-chief of the Combined Armies. The Duke's prowess on the battlefield gave rise to a well-known children's nursery rhyme:"The grand old Duke of York/He had ten thousand men/He marched them up to the top of the hill/And marched them down again."

£500-700

PRATTWARE

Prattware, made in Staffordshire and Yorkshire in the late 18th and early 19th centuries, derives its name from Felix Pratt, one of the best-known makers of this type of earthenware. Items are usually made in a light-coloured clay and decorated with onglaze enamels in a distinctive palette of ochre, green, orange, blue and yellow. The most popular items were relief moulded jugs which often feature military subjects of the day such as Admiral Nelson, surrounded by decorative floral borders.

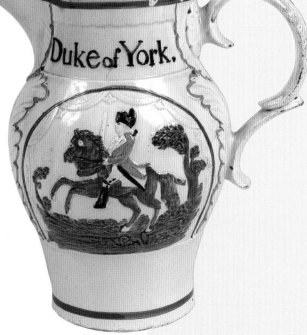

The Golden Jubilee
(1809)

George III was the first king since Edward III to be on the throne for 50 years. He was by far the most popular with his subjects of all the Georges and led a relatively pious and scandal-free life, taking a strong interest in agriculture and animal husbandry. The most desirable jubilee commemoratives are creamware jugs printed with verses recording the Liverpool Amnesty, which pardoned deserters from the navy – deserters from the army were still pardoned only if they reformed.

▼ Like the majority of wares that bear the Liverpool "Amnesty Print", this creamware mug was made at the Herculaneum factory in Liverpool. The black printed decoration shows the Spirit of History and Britannia seated on the clouds supporting a scroll bearing the inscription "Happy Would England be, Could George live to see Another Jubilee". Underneath it is a cipher which bears the words "GIII R 50" and above a scene of prisoners walking out of a prison, encaptioned "Let the Prisoners Go Free". The statue of the Liver bird is taken from the original erected in Liverpool to honour the Jubilee. The Herculaneum factory used the Liver bird as its mark after 1833.

£800-1,200

▼ An earlier version of this pearlware punch bowl appeared with an anti-Jacobin verse incorporated into the decoration. However, it was later adapted to

celebrate the King's jubilee. The inside is decorated with a transfer printed portrait of the King, and on the outside is the motto "King revered and Queen beloved long may they reign". The border decoration emulates that on Chinese export porcelain and there is also Chinoiserie decoration (Chinese motifs, often with a certain fantasy element) on the outside. Like most pearlware, this piece is unmarked.

£400-800

▲ This punchbowl is a variation on the one on the left. It carries the same motto, but with a slightly different print – the portrait of the King is placed within a beaded medallion and has a laurel surround. This example is less desirable as it does not feature the brown edge and the print is not of such high quality. The bowls were probably made in Staffordshire, and were both decorative and functional – no doubt they were used to drink a toast to the King in the jubilee year.

£500-600

▲ This silver figure of George III on a pillar is based on a statue erected at Nocton in Lincolnshire by Robert the 4th Earl of Buckinghamshire in 1810 to commemorate the King's jubilee. The stamp on the base attributes the figure to Paul Storr from Rundell, Bridge and Rundell, 1811. It was the property of Sir Joseph Banks, a botanist and close friend of the King, known today as the father of Australia as he settled at Botany Bay in 1788 and became the country's first governor. The pillar bears his family arms.

◀ This Coalport jardinière inscribed "A Token From Margate" is one of the earliest seaside souvenirs . The silhouette portrait, popular throughout the King's reign, was used by Coalport on a number of their other wares. £600-800

THE MARY ANNE CLARK SCANDAL

At the time of George's jubilee in 1809 scandal broke out around the affair between the king's brother, Frederick, Duke of York, and his mistress Mary Anne Clarke. The Duke was forced to leave the army (although he was later reinstated by the Prince Regent) after it was publicly discovered that Mary had been selling military commissions and promotions. There are numerous rather unflattering pieces recording this event, and the public's disapproval reflects the growing intolerance towards immorality in the early 19th century.

▼ The black print on this creamware jug shows Mary Clarke at the time of investigation by the Parliamentary Commission. Unlike many pieces, it is sympathetic to the Duke and his mistress – the inscription boldly describes her as "Mrs Clarke the late favourite lady of His Royal Highness The Duke of York".

£600-800

The Peninsular Campaign

The peace treaty signed in 1802 in Amiens between England, France, Spain and Holland lasted only 18 months. In 1805 Admiral Nelson fought the Battle of Trafalgar, vanquishing the Franco-Spanish fleet of 33 ships and taking 20,000 prisoners, but losing his life in the process. The battle confirmed Britain's naval supremacy; Nelson became a national hero and his death was commemorated in vast range of wares. Arthur Wellesly, Duke of Wellington (1769-1852), became the next national hero when he took his troops to the aid of the Spanish to defeat the French on land in the Peninsular War in Spain in 1809. Among the events commemorated from this war are the death of the British general, Sir John Moore at the Battle of Corunna in 1809, and the numerous British victories. In 1815 Wellington led the British and allied forces to Waterloo where they defeated the French under Napoleon Bonaparte who had recently fled from exile on the island of Elba. Napoleon was subsequently held captive on the island of St Helena, sailing there on the *HMS Northumberland*, and there are many printed wares which were produced in Sunderland depicting this ship. Figural pieces depicting the leaders were particularly popular. A large quantity of porcelain jugs and plates was also produced, printed in single colours of sepia, blue or black; multi-coloured printing is far rarer.

▼ The decoration on this Staffordshire jug, printed in black and coloured with hand-applied enamels, shows on one side Nelson being mourned and on the other, the figure of Britannia.

£400-500

▲ Jugs, produced posthumously, depicting Wellington, abounded after his victories in Spain and at Waterloo. This relief moulded jug is decorated with a title portrait of Lord Wellington in colonel's uniform; on the back is an almost identical portrait captioned General Hill. This example is of relatively high quality, but many other inferior pieces were made.

£200-300

▼ Few wares were made to celebrate the peace of Paris in 1802. This porcelain cup and saucer is decorated with the Dove of Peace.

£500-700

▲ This Staffordshire earthenware tankard shows the Duke of Wellington on his horse, Copenhagen. The detail of the inside shows salamanders moulded in high relief. Although frog motifs are found inside many tankards, salamanders are a novelty – it is likely that they represent a pun on the word "Salamanca", the scene of one of Wellington's celebrated victories in the Peninsula conflict.

£500-800

BEWARE

▼ A number of copies of prattware jugs have been produced in the 20th century. These can be distinguished from the originals by the duller tone of the pratt colours (red, blue and green) and the over-accentuated crackling on the body. Bases have often been artificially aged which makes them look too dirty. The body of this Nelson mug copy lacks the blue tint found on originals.

£5

◀ This pearlware teapot celebrates Nelson's victory at Trafalgar. The naval aspect is highlighted by the motifs of mermen and anchors. Chips on the rim halve the value. **£250-300**

▲ No item was considered too humble to commemorate the French wars. This redprinted cotton kerchief is printed with the battle scenes at Waterloo and maps of the area.

£650

STAFFORDSHIRE FIGURES

These were developed by the Staffordshire potters in the late 18th century for the working classes, as a more affordable alternative to the expensive porcelain figures decorating the homes of the rich. Before the invention of photography they provided the closest representation of contemporary people, and few celebrities were not modelled as a Staffordshire figure. The figures are decorated in bold high-temperature colours of blue, brown, red and green and although rather crudely modelled, were very popular.

◀ Napoleon Bonaparte was probably the most popular subject for Staffordshire figures, produced in even larger quantities than figures of Wellington. This example dates from 1850, after his death. It is made from a porcellaneous material which is somewhere between bone china and pottery. Bases tend to be hollow and the pieces are often slipcast.

£100-150

The Death of Princess Charlotte
(1817)

Born in 1796, Princess Charlotte was the daughter of George, the Prince of Wales (later George IV) and Queen Caroline, and granddaughter of George III. She was much loved by the British public, who saw her as the saving grace of her ludicrously mismatched parents. She fell in love with and married Prince Leopold of Saxe Coburg on 2 May 1816 and the couple lived in Claremount House, a gift from the nation. Their wedding and move to Claremont are commemorated in a number of brightly-coloured wares. Tragically, Charlotte died in childbirth on 5 November 1817, leaving the country to grieve her and her stillborn baby. Her death is said to have contributed largely to George III's madness. Charlotte's popularity is reflected in the large number of items commemorating her death.

▼ This blue and white transfer printed plate shows the Princess in an advanced state of pregnancy, and must therefore date from c. 1817, just before her untimely death. Prince Leopold and Charlotte are depicted in landscaped grounds, enjoying a walk.

Their chance meeting with an old woman and boy underlines the couple's endearing accessibility to the general public. The plate is marked "British Views" and was probably one of a series.

£150-200

▲ Apsley Pellatt introduced the *crystallo ceramie* method of decoration to England, which had originated in France in the 18th century. It involved integrating into the glass a decorative panel which could withstand greater heat than molten glass. Often Pellatt used a ceramic panel. The portrait of the Princess is after a painting by Challon. This is one of only a very few pieces of Charlotte memorabilia executed in glass. The enamelled coroneted funerary urn flanked by a willow and rose support the fact it was made after her death.

£600-800

◀ One of the most popular subjects with Staffordshire potters was the meeting of the Prince and Princess with an old woman called Goody Bewley. When the royal couple met the woman outside her cottage trying to read the small print of a bible they gave her a quarto edition of the book. This cup and saucer depict the encounter that warmed the hearts of the British public.

£250-300

LUSTRE WARES

Pink lustre was often found on the rims of commemorative wares in the 18th century and was particularly popular with the Staffordshire and Sunderland potters. It is otherwise known as purple or manganese lustre, and varies in tone from pink to purple.

▼ Among the more unusual items commemorating Princess Charlotte's death

is this Staffordshire enamelled box. The dark blue base and top incorporate a white reserve panel painted with a naive design showing Britannia mourning the Princess's death.

£1,000

▼ The decoration on this cup and saucer produced to commemorate the death of Princess Charlotte is fairly typical of the time – the allegorical figures of Britannia and Faith mourning at the tomb of the Princess were popular motifs on funerary wares and appear on a whole host of royal commemoratives. The rim edged in pink lustre suggests that the set was probably made in Staffordshire. **£150-200**

▲ This black printed saucer dish with a pink lustre rim is decorated with an oval portrait medallion of the young Princess Charlotte. Made by an unknown Staffordshire potter, it probably formed part of a tea service. A similar print is also found on a jug alongside a complementary portrait of Prince Leopold.

£120-180

Madness and Death

George III suffered from porphyria which led to periods of madness. His first significant bout in 1788 caused a political crisis, as the Whig government attempted to have the king's oldest son, the Prince of Wales, declared Regent. The King's madness and restoration to health the following year were popular with the Staffordshire potters. Unfortunately, the King lapsed into permanent madness in 1810 which plagued him for the ten years leading up to his death in 1820. He went blind and deaf and became obsessed with the idea of purity; he insisted on wearing white robes and believed he was Shakespeare's King Lear. He was a sensitive man and his death was probably also affected by the death of his youngest daughter Amelia and his disapproval of his son's debauched lifestyle. The King was sadly mourned which is evident by the wide range of commemoratives available.

▼ This child's plate depicts the King as the caring personality he was popularly known to be and shows the public's loyalty to him. Moulded with a laurel garland and printed in sepia, it is typical of children's plates at the time. Variations exist with different floral borders and with a blue print, which tends to be a little more desirable. Others were decorated in Pratt colours (see p. 41). The inscription quotes the King when he met Joseph Lancaster who set up the Lancasterian schools for the underpriveleged. These were strongly allied to the Church and had the King as their patron. These plates were probably made for distribution among the schools.

£850

▼ A number of wares were produced to celebrate the King's temporary return to health in 1789. This creamware footed jug is a fine example. The patriotic verse "Britons rejoyce Cheer

up and Sing, And Drink to His Health, Long Live the King" exemplifies the enthusiasm with which the event was greeted and shows the country's obvious affection for the Monarch. Surrounding the portrait medallion are military trophies, royal beasts and arms, all transfer printed in brick-red. The piece is dated March 17, 1789, 21 years before the King's final bout of madness from which he never recovered.

£600-800

▼ This very rare pearlware bowl is another example of the wares produced to celebrate the King's recovery to health in 1789. It bears a similarly patriotic inscription to that on the jug on the left – "Britons rejoice in this grand thing/Protect your Country and your King". It is interesting to see the figure of Britannia on such an early piece; on later examples she is regularly shown wearing a plumed hat.

£800-1,000

▲ The cornucopia and agricultural implements on the border of this platter are an allusion to George III's nickname "Farmer George", earned through his keen and often comical love of country pursuits. The plate was made by Davenport in Staffordshire, who specialized in blue transfer printed earthenware, and is part of a complete dinner service.

£700-800

▲ It is rare to find pieces which feature only Queen Charlotte. This pearlware punch bowl was made in the early 19th century and was probably produced out of sympathy for the Queen, who was severely distressed at the outset of the King's madness.

£700-800

► Plates specifically commemorating George's death are rare and command a premium. This design is relatively simple, with a funeral black printed transfer of the King in military uniform, bearing an inscription to his sacred memory.

£500-800

George IV
(1820 - 1830)

George IV, the eldest son of George III, was Regent for nine years before becoming King in 1820. Father and son constantly fell out, largely because of the son's immorality and inability to control his financial affairs. The new King was a fashionable and good-looking man, famous for his love of women and his flamboyant lifestyle which got him into increasing debt. He married the one true love in his life, Mrs Fitzherbert, in 1785 but the contract was declared null and void as it contravened the Royal Marriages Act. After numerous affairs and under increasing pressure from family and advisors to settle down, he finally made the ill-fated marriage to Caroline of Brunswick in 1885. Both partners detested each other from the start, and it is reputed that the King was outrageously drunk at the ceremony, as this was the only way he could go ahead with the wedding. The couple separated shortly afterwards and the King's notorious attempts to divorce his wife, culminating in the famous Green Bag Affair (see pp. 52-3), made him very unpopular with the public. Although not really interested in politics, the King changed upon his coronation to support the Whigs rather than the Tories who had been in Parliament during his father's reign. He did not approve of reform and only consented to the passing of the Catholic Emancipation Act in 1829 (which allowed Catholics into Parliament and public office) as he realised he was powerless to prevent it. George IV's redeeming feature was his love of the Arts, to which he gave great financial support; he had a vast collection of paintings, many of which are now in London's National Gallery, and he loved the theatre and literature. His passion for architecture is manifested in the buildings he commissioned. Many, like the Brighton Pavilion were designed by John Nash, in the architectural style which has now been given the name of Regency after the King's earlier title of Prince Regent.

Any commemoratives made for George IV's ascension and coronation are vastly overshadowed by the wealth of wares made to mark the scandal of the Green Bag Affair, and consequently any pieces made for George's coronation are highly collectable. Transfer printing had established itself as the most cost effective way of decorating ceramics and such wares, made for the masses, were produced on a wide scale for the Green Bag Affair. Other pieces were made in bone china, including a bat printed tea service for the Princess Charlotte's death. In addition to transfer printed decoration, pink lustre often appeared on rims, spouts and bases of jugs, mugs and plates. The motif of Britannia, used by the Romans to represent Great Britain, became popular at a time when neo-classicism was experiencing a new vogue. She had already appeared on coins in the reign of George III, and the reign of George IV saw a lasting association of Britannia with mourning wares, where she is seen weeping at the tombs of various leading figures and monarchs. Although ceramics still dominated the commemorative scene, other media were used. Inspired by the decoration on Wedgwood's jasperware, models in wax, a less expensive alternative to porcelain, became popular, as did glass medallion portraits set into glass by designers James and William Tassie.

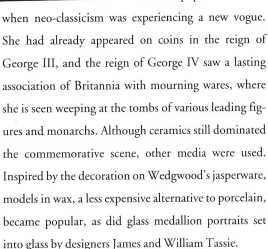

Left: A pink wax profile portrait of Queen Caroline, c.1820.

Above: A Regency gold portrait snuff box by Alexander Strachan, with a miniature of the Prince Regent, London 1818.

Queen Caroline and the Green Bag Affair

King George III arranged the marriage of his son to Caroline of Brunswick as the Prince had incurred massive debts which Parliament would only pay off if he married. Mutual dislike led the couple to split up only three months after the birth of their daughter, Charlotte in 1796. Caroline's ensuing amorous liaisons caused embarrassment to the King, and following advice to flee abroad, she went to live with her lover Count Bergami at the Villa d'Este on the shores of Lake Como in Italy, from where she proceeded to slander her husband's name. Rumours of her behaviour led the King to send a Royal Commission to Milan to find out what was going on. All the evidence was collected and brought back to England at the time that the Prince became King, in 1820. To try and prevent Caroline from becoming Queen the King brought a Bill of Pains and Penalties against her, the evidence for which was collected in a green baize bag. After a long trial and a huge scandal the Bill was refuted. The couple's ill-fated marriage produced some of the most amusing and unusual commemoratives, and various items were decorated with satirical rhymes referring to the famous "green bag" court case.

▲ Typically, this jug refers to Caroline as Queen although she was never crowned – the doors of Westminster Abbey were barred against her upon the orders of the King. Green Bag jugs came in graduated sizes. The decoration is typical – printed in black with the upper parts covered in a copper lustre glaze and lined with a pink burnish. **£400-500**

▼ This pro-Caroline mug depicts a cartoon of the duelling couple seated on the scales of justice. The inscription "A Good Piece of Wood" refers to Alderman Wood, Lord Mayor of London, who was one of her staunchest supporters. **£500-600**

▲ The bust portrait of Caroline featured on this Prattware jug appears on a number of wares. The satyr mask lip was popular on drinking vessels. **£300-400**

◄ The scalloped edge and feathered decoration of this plate was very fashionable during this period. The blue profile portrait is transfer printed with the caption "Long Live Queen Caroline!" inscribed in highly ornate lettering, reflecting support for the wronged Caroline.

£250-300

WAX MODELS

Fakes abound in wax items, especially those depicting Nelson and Wellington. Fraudulent pieces can be spotted by careful scrutiny of the lettering and the hand colouring – which is usually not as meticulous as in authentic examples. One of the finest wax modellers was Samuel Percy who created very realistic portraits in high relief of a number of leading personalities.

▼ In 1820 Queen Caroline was examined for her licentious behaviour. The dramatic events during the trial are portrayed in this mezzotint steel engraving by J. Bromley and J. Porter. The House of Lords is packed to the rafters as only Catholics, the recently bereaved and the seriously ill were allowed to absent themselves from the proceedings. The costly three-month proceeding was followed closely by the public, and when the case against Caroline was dismissed the result was greeted with great enthusiasm. Her victory resulted in a huge decline in the King's popularity.

£50-60

► Wax was a popular medium for profile miniatures and was relatively inexpensive. This example, dated c.1820, has very fine detail in the modelling of the features of the troubled Queen. Although this piece is unsigned, it retains a high value because of the splendid workmanship. The same portrait appears on the jug on the left; the feathered top hat is characteristic of Caroline's flamboyant attire.

£1,200

The Coronation
(1820)

All events in the life of George IV tend to be over-shadowed by the scandal surrounding himself and his estranged wife, Caroline. Consequently, although a large amount of wares were produced to mark this affair (see pp. 52-3, Queen Caroline and the Green Bag), coronation pieces are rare – and therefore highly collectable. The King was unpopular and was seen as a decadent philanderer – his love of show was manifested in the Brighton pavilion which he commissioned to be built. In contrast, Caroline was much-loved, and potters frequently portrayed her as Queen even though this title was denied her by the King. Very few pieces show the couple together. A large number of coronation items have been decorated using the bat-printing method which was popularized during this period.

◄ Wax portrait busts were very popular at this time. This example of George IV would originally have been encased in a glass dome. The wax plinth bears the inscription "London, Published by C. Flint, May 1828 D. Morison Fecit". It exists as a pair with a bust of the Duke of Kent.

£200-300 each

▼ The mark of the Liverpool-based Herculaneum factory is impressed on the base of these two rare and important plaques. The factory produced lustre ware, terracotta and some porcelain, but was best known for its range of creamware jugs, often black printed with designs from outside factories. These plaques are printed in puce –one shows George seated on the throne in his coronation robes; the other has a floral cartouche encircling the words "God Save the King". Their value is high as no other pairs are known to exist.

£2,000 the pair

BAT PRINTING

The bat printing method enabled monochrome prints to be applied over the glaze. Developed in Staffordshire in the late 1760s it involved transferring a print from a copper engraving onto an object in oil using a seal of glue or gelatine (bat). The print was then dusted with powdered colour pigments and the piece was fired in a kiln so that the oil vaporized and the pigments fused to the glaze.

▲ The name of Apsley Pellat, the maker of this scent flask, became synonymous with the technique of insetting glass with medallions, and their wares provided a good alternative to the portrait medallions made by Wedgwood (see p. 37). The medallion on the front of the bottle portrays George IV as a Roman Emperor and the medallion on the reverse his coronation. The decoration on this piece is very elaborate and reflects the change in glass styles from the reign of George III, when cutting was much more restrained. The medallion, particularly because of its royal subject, increases the price of the flask dramatically; without it the piece would be worth only half the price.

£2,000-2,500

▲ This rare small beaker marks the coronation that never happened, as Caroline is wearing a crown. The bat-printed portrait shows sympathy to the Princess by presenting her as younger than her 53 years. The strong pink lustre trim is of high quality and although slightly chipped this piece is worth at least £400.

▲ This vase was made as part of a series which also featured William Pitt and Lord Castlereagh. The royal subject makes it highly desirable. The hand-painted colourful portrait of the King is quite flattering, making him look more youthful than his years. The rather bizarre decoration adorning his coat is significant as he saw himself as a fashion designer – he designed several military uniforms. Because the piece is quite rare it was estimated to fetch £600-800, but in fact it made £1,300!

▼ The bat printed portrait of Caroline on this Staffordshire jug was first used on a mug to mark the death of Princess Charlotte in 1817! The blue-tinted glaze and oviform shape were popular in Staffordshire.

£300-400

The Deaths of Caroline and George IV

The fiasco of Caroline turning up at Westminster Abbey in 1821 in an attempt to be crowned alongside her estranged husband has often been referred to as her death blow as she died 16 days later. However, contrary to the romantic belief that Caroline died of a broken heart from this rejection, she in fact died from abdominal problems and over-medication, although a lowering of her spirits may have contributed. A whole range of pieces were produced lamenting her death and showing solidarity with the injured Queen. According to her wishes she was buried at the family vault at Brunswick and this scene has become the subject of prints on plates, jugs, mugs and of hand-coloured mezzo tints; other pieces often show Britannia weeping at her tomb.

King George IV ruled for nine years before his untimely death in 1830, which was hastened by the excesses of his lifestyle. Unusually, more pieces were made for his death than for his coronation. The Staffordshire potters in particular were keen to produce memorial pieces. However, the majority of these memorial commemoratives tend to show little variety.

▼ **Tombs** frequently appear on wares mourning the death of Queen Caroline, but the particular design on this porcelain mug is extremely desirable as no other examples have been recorded. The colourfull enamelled decoration includes willow trees encircling the Queen's tomb which are emblematic of death. The inscription pays homage to the "wronged" Queen and reads "In Memory of Caroline of Brunswick. The Injured Queen of England Died August 7th, 1821 at Hammer-smith (sic) and Buried the 23rd, at Brunswick Aged 53".

£600-800

▲ **Bat printed creamware jugs** were popular commemoratives (see p. 55). They often sported the pink lustre trim which decorates this example mourning the death of Queen Caroline. The print shows the figure of Britannia weeping at the Queen's tomb, much used for wares commemorating the deaths of Caroline and her daughter.

£300-400

▼ Not all portraits of Caroline were flattering – the sepia-coloured print on this plate is particularly unattractive. It shows the Princess wearing a characteristically elaborate hat, suggestive of her wayward lifestyle. The maker is unknown but the piece would seem to have been made by someone unsympathetic to Caroline's plight.

£250-350

▲ Black and purple were popular funeral colours in the 19th century. The printed design on this jug shows the head and shoulder portrait of the King reversed with a memorium script giving details of his ascension, proclamation and death. The shape, typically elaborate, echoes silver styles of the day and reflects the growing Rococo revival. The piece is marked with the initials GBH, the mark of Goodwin Bridgwood and Harris of Staffordshire who are particularly noted for their production of early 19th century commemoratives.

£250-350

► Only the presence of angels on this jug make it recognizable as a memorial piece. This type of stoneware, known as drabware, was popular from c.1830-50, but it was an unusual medium for commemoratives. The decorative handle depicts a lion moulded in low relief. The piece is known to have been made in three sizes. The portrait has darkened and lost some of its definition through age but the jug is still valuable.

£250-350

▲ Although this jug was also made by Goodwin Bridgwood and Harris, it is more elaborate in form and the print is different – the king has a more pronounced tousled coiffure. Puce is slightly more desirable than black and this and the more ornate handle and form increases the price.

£400-500

TREACLE PAINTINGS

A number of fine hand-coloured mezzo tints were produced for the death of Caroline. These record the depositing of the body in the family vault at Brunswick on 24 August 1821 or Britannia weeping at the Queen's tomb. These pictures are often called treacle paintings becaue of their strong brown colours.

▼ This mezzotint of Britannia mourning at the Queen's tomb was published on 1 October 1821 by P&P Gally.

£100-150

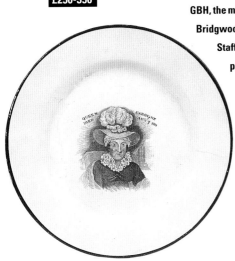

William IV

(1830 - 1837)

After ten years of rule by George III's son George IV, the public were not at all happy when his third son, Prince William Henry, came to the throne in 1830, as they feared the same bad leadership as from the previous Georges. However, their fears were unfounded, and the new King proved to be an astute and shrewd leader at a politically difficult time. William was known as the "Sailor Prince" or "Sailor Bill" because of his strong naval background – he went to sea at the age of 14, was a great friend and admirer of Admiral Nelson, and served with Admiral Rodney during the American War of Independence in his father's reign. He was 65 when he came to the throne and he brought with him the hearty character he had developed at sea. His good nature and public display of clean living and fidelity soon earned him the respect of his subjects, and his happy "love" marriage to Adelaide of Saxe-Meiningen in 1818 was much welcomed. In earlier years he had lived with the actress Mrs Jordan with whom he had fathered ten children.

William's reign was a period of severe poverty for the country – at the King's coronation, which is often referred to as the "half-crownation", there was no horse procession from Westminster Abbey and no state banquet, and it is alleged that Queen Adelaide even had to provide the jewels for her own crown. William's reign was dominated by political unrest and social reform, which culminated in the passing of the Reform Act in 1832 under Lord Grey (although only begrudgingly passed by the King). The great philanthropist Lord Shaftesbury fought constantly to reduce the misery caused by the industrial revolution and to improve the plight of the poor. He introduced, among other acts, the Factory Act of 1833, which banned all children under 9 years of age from working in factories. 1833 was also the year that the Anti-Slavery Act was passed, which abolished slavery throughout the British Empire.

Because of the public's initial lack of enthusiasm for the new King, and the country's poverty, relatively few items were made for William's ascension, coronation or death, and they are highly desirable. A few wares were produced for the coronation and these were decorated with portraits of both the King and Queen, but by far the most commemorated event was the passing of the Reform Act. This gave potters the opportunity to spread propagandist feeling throughout the nation, by printing political mottoes on their wares. As with the previous reigns of George III and George IV, most items were transfer-printed pottery, usually in monochrome, but occasionally decorated with coloured onglaze enamels and pink lustre; others were totally covered in a pink wash. Pottery forms started to veer away from the neo-classical shapes of George IV's reign towards a Rococo revival; the potteries in Staffordshire and Coalbrookdale made some floral encrusted wares with elaborate borders. The dearth of commemoratives for William's reign, reflecting a loss of tolerance for George III's sons, is in stark contrast to the abundance of wares made for the King's young niece, Victoria, who came to the throne upon the death of the King who, ironically, had failed to father a legitimate heir with Queen Adelaide.

Left: A treacle glazed pottery wall plaque celebrating the abolition of slavery in 1833.

Above: A large octagonal plate for William IV's coronation, 1830.

The Coronation
(1831)

William IV ascended the throne with his wife Queen Adelaide in 1830 , following the death of his brother George IV who did not leave an heir. The event is marked by relatively few commemoratives and therefore any wares are highly desirable. The coronation on 8 September of the following year enjoyed wider acclaim and led to several different types of pottery being made, the majority of them in Staffordshire. Some pieces portray the King and Queen in their coronation robes; others depict them dressed less formally – some even show the King wearing a lace ruff. There are also items showing the coronation procession. Most pottery was made by unknown makers and was usually decorated with transfer prints. Any pieces by a known maker command a premium. Elaborate borders were particularly popular, as were Rococo-style handles. Other decoration included pink wash glazes and pink lustre rims, overglaze hand painting and enamels. Many images of the King and Queen were re-used, so any rarer prints are more desirable. Items showing the couple enthroned are particularly sought-after, as are hand-enamelled plates with moulded portraits of the couple encircled in a border.

▲ The pink lustre wash on this large Staffordshire mug makes the piece very desirable. Very unusually for the period, the print of the King and Queen in their coronation robes is signed by the engraver. The inside is decorated with the flowers of the union of England, Scotland and Wales.

£400-500

▼ Although this mug was made for William IV's accession, similar mugs were issued with the word "Reform" in the crown for the passing of the Reform Act of 1832. The lustre band around the base and the thick potting suggest it was made in Scotland.

£500

◄ The lattice and flowerhead background on this stoneware mug can be found on a a number of other commemorative wares produced by Minton at this time, including another version of this jug made in white earthenware. The applied decoration is slightly discoloured, suggesting an imperfection in the appliqué and this will lower the value. William IV appears on the front; on the reverse is a similar portrait of Adelaide.

£400

► These wax busts of William and Adelaide were modelled by C. Flint; other examples by him include George IV (see p. 54). They would originally have been encased in glass domes for display. Other examples of wax miniatures were made in profile and enhanced with facial tints and painted attire. These were often mounted on wooden backgrounds and cased in glass to be hung on walls.

£400-600

► The silhouette portrait print of William on this jug is the only prints so far recorded to appear on wares made to commemorate the King's accession to the throne. The same print also appears on a number of plates produced for the event.

£350-450

▼ This wall plaque commemorating the coronation has a portrait of Queen Adelaide transfer-printed in pink. Originally, it was probably one of a pair with a portrait of William. The piece bears the impressed mark for the Southwick pottery in Sunderland.

£400-600

▲ This Staffordshire pottery jug is particularly interesting because, unusually, it shows William at the coronation ceremony at Westminster Abbey – a fine tureen also exists bearing a similar print. The inside rim of the jug is decorated with the royal coat of arms.

£300-400

◄ This print of William is one of the most popular – examples also exist in black, brown and pink. The discoloration of the porous cream body lowers the value from £200 to £150.

Social & Political Upheaval

Political unrest during the reign of William IV finally led to the passing of the Reform Bill in 1832. The Bill was introduced by Lord John Russell under Lord Grey's Whig government to make parliamentary democracy more representative by abolishing obsolete constituencies and granting more seats to the industrial centres, and giving greater representation to the lower classes. It also abolished "rotten" or "pocket boroughs", owned by landowners and members of parliament who used their power to trade boroughs for seats. The Bill was initially defeated in the Commons, and even when passed at the second attempt, it did not pass through the Lords until Lord Grey went to see William IV and proposed the appointment of enough new peers in favour of the Bill to ensure its passage. In the end this was unnecessary as the Bill was accepted under Tory submission, led by the Duke of Wellington. Key figures of reform at this time were Lord Grey, Lord Althorp, Lord Brougham and Lord Russell, all of whom appeared on a variety of commemoratives.

▼ The print on this Staffordshire pottery plate shows William IV addressing and threatening to dissolve parliament, and was typical of the mass of political and satirical cartoons which circulated in this period. Entitled "Dissolution of Parliament", it illustrates an unlikely threat, as William was not keen on reform. A similar print appears on jugs and punch bowls.

£200-300

▲ Earl Grey and Lord Russell appear on this jug entitled "Champions of Reform". The decorative border features the flowers of union, representing Britain's unity. The piece was made by Goodwin Bridgwood and Harris, and the shape of the body and the distinctive foliate handle are typical of this maker (see also p. 57). Their wares are marked and command a premium.

£250-350

◀ Lord Brougham entered Parliament in 1810 as a Whig and was actively involved in many reforms, including the abolition of the slave trade and lifting trade restrictions with the Continent. It is as Lord Chancellor that he appears on this jug celebrating his achievements. Slight damage lowers the value.

£300-400

▲ Bourne Potteries in Derbyshire made stoneware gimmel flasks, many of which were modelled as various figures involved in the Reform Bill. Flasks were a popular vehicle for expressing political allegiance.

£200

THE CORN LAWS AND THE PETERLOO MASSACRE

A major source of discontent was the passing of the Corn Laws in 1815 which although protecting British farmers by placing high duties on imported grain, kept the British price high and made bread very expensive. In 1819 the activist Henry Hunt led a peaceful gathering of over 60,000 men, women and children at St Peter's Field in Manchester to petition Parliament for the repeal of the Corn Laws. Under orders of the magistrates the meeting was charged by cavalry and 11 people were killed and over 400 injured. The event became known as the Peterloo massacre.

▲ This Staffordshire jug is decorated with a naive but interesting print. The inscription of "The Old Rotten Tree" on the reverse refers to the Rotten Boroughs system. The four men assaulting the tree with an axe represent the Whigs Grey, Althorp, Brougham and Russell.

£400-600

◀ This very rare jug was one of the earliest pottery items to mark the Peterloo massacre and show support for the repeal of the Corn Laws. An inscription on a penant reads "Hunt for Ever", referring to the hero of the demonstration who was imprisoned for two years for his part in organising the rally.

Victoria
(1838 - 1901)

Victoria's reign was a period of great political and social reform. In 1839 there was threat of a General Strike; Chartists set out to achieve political reform for the masses and almost caused a revolution in the late 1840s; in 1846 the Anti Corn Law league managed to persuade Robert Peel to repeal the corn laws, but not before millions died of starvation in Ireland in the potato famines; there was a Tory split in government and the Liberals emerged under William Gladstone and the Conservatives under Victoria's favourite Prime Minister Benjamin Disraeli; there were wars in the Crimea, the Sudan, Zululand, South Africa and Ireland; the second Reform Act was passed by Disraeli in 1867, paving the way for a number of other Acts, including the Education Act (1870), the Trade Union

Act (1871) and the Ballot Act (1872); and in 1880 Gladstone gave Ireland home rule.

The young Victoria was seen as a refreshing contrast to the sons of George III, and her accession and coronation were greeted with a wealth of commemoratives. Transfer-printed pottery dominated at the time of Victoria's coronation in 1838; those from South Wales tend to be more desirable than those from Staffordshire. Brown saltglaze stonewares were popular – moulded jugs and gin flasks that depicted the masters of reform in William's reign now adopted the image of Victoria. Her marriage in 1840 to her cousin, Albert of Saxe-Coburg was celebrated profusely by the Staffordshire potteries, primarily in jugs and mugs. Albert was well-liked, and his greatest contribution to the country, the Great Exhibition of 1851, spawned a host of collectables. When he died in 1861 the market was inundated with memorial wares transfer printed in black or purple, but then there was a void as Victoria retired from public life and there was serious talk of abolishing the monarchy and forming a republic. Victoria became Empress of India in 1877 and a few Empire plates were made asserting the country's

stronghold on the world, but it was not until her re-emergence at her Golden Jubilee in 1887 that confidence was restored in the Crown. More commemoratives were produced for her Diamond Jubilee than ever before. This jubilee also marked the progression from black and white to colour transfer-printed wares. Victoria died in 1901 and the event was met with great sadness and disbelief. For such a long and adventurous reign there were very few memorial wares made. Parian busts of Victoria and Albert were popular, as were Staffordshire figures, flat-backs and relief-moulded jugs. Pottery shapes were more elaborate, continuing the Rococo revival of ealier years – cups had exuberant handles and plates had lavish decorative borders. Loving cups were fashionable – those by Copeland are among some of the finest collectables of Victoria's reign. Woven silk pictures known as Stevengraphs feature the Queen's portrait and, following the development of the cine camera, a whole range of printed ephemera was produced which is available at relatively low prices. The popularity of cigarette smoking led to the emergeance of cigarette cards, many of which feature the Queen and events from her reign.

Left: A Staffordshire figure of Queen Victoria 11¼in (29cm) high, c.1855.

Above: A brown glazed stoneware Doulton figure of Queen Victoria by John Broad, c.1901.

Accession and Coronation

The accession (1837) and coronation (1838) of Victoria were greeted with enormous enthusiasm by the British public. Her accession had been far from trouble free. William IV hated Victoria's mother the Duchess of Kent (his sister-in-law) and knew that if he died before Victoria's 18th birthday the Duchess would become Regent. Despite his illness, he managed to survive for a month after Victoria's birthday, thus cheating the Duchess of the power she craved. Behind the scenes the Duchess and her advisors tried to encourage Victoria to agree to let her mother rule until her 21st birthday, but Victoria was astute enough to evade all such attempts and when William died on June 1837 she became Queen without further ado.

Victoria's huge popularity is reflected in the number of items produced for her ascension. Most were inexpensive transfer-printed wares from Swansea or Staffordshire which when made would have cost only a few pence. Popular portraits by artists such as Sir George Hayter and Henry Collen were adapted for the purpose. The same image was used by many different potters but the better quality wares are more skilfull in their decoration.

▼ The print of Queen Victoria on this Staffordshire milk jug appears with varying degrees of quality on a wide number of wares made to commemorate the Queen's coronation. The print on the reverse is accompanied by a moral verse promoting temperance ("The Drunkard Shall Not Enter the Kingdom of God"), and is characteristic of the morality that was imposed upon the people in Victorian England.

£300-400

▲ The portrait of the Queen on this Read and Clementson mug is after an original painting by Sir George Hayter. On the reverse is a portrait of the Duchess of Kent, who appears on many of Victoria's coronation and ascension pieces before her marriage to Albert. The fine quality printing and design, coupled with the maker's mark on the base, are reflected in this jug's value.

£600-800

▼ A number of towns commissioned their own mugs to commemorate Victoria's accession and coronation. This blue-printed Davenport mug was made for the town of Preston and bears the

inscription "Success to the Town and Trade of Preston". Its rarity increases its value and makes it a very collectable item.

£600-800

▼ An extensive range of plates was made for Victoria's accession to the throne, many of which bear the popular portrait taken from an original by Sir George Hayter which appears on the jug on the previous page. The portrait of the young Queen Victoria printed on this plate made in Swansea by the Dillwyn and Co. pottery is less flattering than Hayter's and makes Victoria look very miserable and rather plump. However, the fine quality of the printing and the attractive border of relief moulded flowers make it still a desirable item for the collector.

£300-400

▲ This saltglaze stoneware gin flask is modelled in the form of the Queen. The reverse is impressed "Queen Alexandrina Victoria", dating it to her acscession: Alexandrina was dropped in favour of Victoria on later examples. Like earlier flasks for the passing of the Reform Act, it bears a patriotic message – the Queen is holding a scroll which reads "Peace and Prosperity Prevail".

£250-350

▼ The busy blue and white decoration on this miniature Staffordshire cream jug makes it particularly attractive. The Hayter portrait of the young Queen appears on both sides.

£250-350

▼ This mug is one of a number of brown and buff stoneware commemoratives that were produced for Queen Victoria's accession to the throne; other items include jugs and gin flasks (see left). The central applied royal coat of arms is flanked by moulded titled bust portraits of Queen Victoria and her mother, the Duchess of Kent.

£300-500

The Royal Wedding and Motherhood
(1840)

Victoria became engaged to her first cousin Albert of Saxe-Cobourg and Gotha in 1839 and married him on 10 February of the following year at the Chapel Royal in St James's Palace. She was given away by her uncle the Duke of Sussex and in her marriage vows she omitted the promise to obey. At first Albert was regarded with suspicion by the British public, largely because of his German descent, and also because he didn't want to invite the Duke of Wellington to his wedding because of his dislike of the Tories (later the two were reconciled and a painting by Winterhalter in 1851 shows Wellington kneeling before the Royal Family). Victoria's wedding gown was in white satin and decorated in Honiton lace – setting a craze for Honiton lace amongst Victorians – and she wore a sapphire brooch. The couple spent their honeymoon at Windsor. On 21 November 1840 Princess Victoria Adelaide Mary Louisa, the first of their nine children, was born, and the Prince of Wales, later Edward VII, was born a year later, in 1841, and these two children became the most favoured subjects for commemoratives.

▲ This tureen is probably one of the largest pieces of early Victorian commemorative pottery made. The green printed portrait of Victoria, commissioned by her mother, is taken from a drawing by F J Lane, engraved by F C Lewis. The shape is typical of that used for tablewares at the time. Other items with the same design include a plate and soup bowl, and it seems likely they were all part of an extensive dinner service. Because it is rare the tureen will command a premium.

£800-1,000

▼ The puce transfer print on this Staffordshire jug shows the Queen in wedding attire with her Consort. Although the reserve panels on this example are in canary yellow, examples also exist in sky blue – yellow is more desirable. The form is typical of this kind of ware in the 1840s, although the handle is a little more exuberant than those usually found.

£300-400

▲ The inscription on this jug to "James Faun 1840", the Farmer's Arms and the animal vignettes all suggest it was presented to a farmer.

£250-350

▼ Early Staffordshire figures like this portrait of Albert tend to be more naively modelled than later ones. The body, of semi-translucent porcelain rather than pottery, was favoured by several Staffordshire potters, particularly Lloyd of Shelton. This piece is one of a pair with the Queen. Most examples are lined with gilding – on earlier examples the gold is honey-coloured; in later examples it is harsher.

£200

ALBERT

▲ This 1850's figure of Albert is far more confident than earlier flatbacks. The high quality gilding and colours confirm its authenticity, even though the deep crazing visible on this piece can be found on 20th-century copies.

£200-300

▼ The Queen's children were presented by the Staffordshire potters in a number of different pursuits. Here the Prince and Princess Royal look particularly endearing, mounted on Shetland ponies – equestrian subjects were rare at this time (c.1846) and are a precursor to the later figures of military commanders on horseback. The scroll-moulded heavy bases are also unusual and soon gave way to simpler bases. The high quality of the decoration is evident in the detail of the children's hair and eyebrows. The colours are typical of this type of figure. These earlier forms of gold lettered title gave way to moulded examples later in the century (see left).

£400-500

Royal Marriages

Although all nine of Queen Victoria's children lived to marry, most commemoratives were made for the weddings of the two eldest children – Victoria, the Princess Royal, and Albert, the Prince of Wales. The first to wed was Victoria, who married Frederick III of Prussia in 1858 at St James's Chapel. The wedding was seen as a fortuitous match strengthening Britain's political alliances. Huge quantities of transfer-printed wares were produced, showing the bride and groom in their wedding regalia – the Princess wore a dress of white moiré trimmed with Honiton lace and the Prince was clad in the uniform of a Prussian general. The marriage of Albert to Princess Alexandra of Denmark was less auspicious. The wedding took place in 1863 at St George's Chapel, Windsor, two years after the death of Prince Albert, when the Queen was in deep mourning. Victoria blamed the scandals surrounding her son's philandering as contributing to her husband's death and refused to attend his wedding, watching instead from Catherine of Aragon's closet, and not appearing for the wedding breakfast. Despite the shadow cast over the wedding a huge variety of items were made in pottery, parian and bone china. Among the most attractive are Staffordshire portrait figures and colour-printed pot lids. Nearly all of these were relatively inexpensive when made, and remain reasonably priced.

◄ One of the most attractive commemoratives made for the wedding of the Prince of Wales and Princess Alexandra is this colour transfer printed plate by Felix Pratt who pioneered the colour printing technique. Even though the pottery has become slightly discoloured the plate is still highly desirable.

£80-120

▼ This unmarked jug was probably made in Staffordshire. Other examples have a picture of the Prussian royal palace on the reverse, taken from an illustration published in the *Illustrated London News*. Although this piece is made in pottery examples also exist in china.

£100-150

▲ The print on this tea plate made for the wedding of Victoria and Frederick is less refined than that on the jug on the left and there is very little detail on the couple's faces. However, the piece is enlivened by the addition of green enamelling (which is a little uncontrolled) and a lustre trim. The same print was used on cups and saucers.

£60-90

◄ This jug was made to celebrate the marriage of Princess Alexandra to Albert. Alexandra's portrait is encircled by snowdrops; on the reverse Albert is shown surrounded by a similar border, made up of oak leaves which are symbolic of England. The type of glaze used on this piece, where the cobalt blue has diffused into the surrounding area, was sometimes known as "flow blue". It was favoured by several Scottish potters, including the firm which made this piece, J & MP Bell & Co. of Clyde .

£275

▲ Many prints depicting the life of Victoria were reproduced in the magazine *Graphics*. This one shows Queen Victoria's marriage to Albert, an event described by the Queen as "the most happy day in my life". **£40-50**

▼ Parian was very popular for small-scale portrait busts in the mid-19th century. This finely modelled bust of the Prince of Wales was made in 1863 to commemorate his wedding.

£200-300

▼ Commemoratives celebrating the marriage of Alfred to Princess Marie of Russia are rare, making this transfer-printed octagonal plate highly desirable. Victoria greeted the marriage with little enthusiasm, but later developed a fondness for her new daughter-in-law, whom she described as "very fresh and attractive".

£450

▲ From c.1879 Thomas Stevens of Coventry made silk pictures on looms using the jacquard machine. Although made by others, they all became known as "Stevengraphs". This silk portrait of Princess Alice was made by Stevens for her wedding to Louis IV of Hesse in 1862. **£60-70**

The Great Exhibition (1851)

The Great Exhibition was primarily a showcase for Industrial Britain, exhibiting what was considered to be the best of British arts and craftsmanship and technology. Together with Henry Cole, Prince Albert conceived the idea of the Exhibition and was an active member of the organizing committee; he also helped to acquire the necessary finances. From the many entries submitted for the design of the building to house the Exhibition, it was Joseph Paxton's Crystal Palace that won – a huge glass and steel structure based on the Lily House at Chatsworth in Derbyshire. It was erected in Hyde Park around the trees and spread over an area of 19 square acres. Among the 13,000 exhibitors over half were British. Although highly successful (and profitable) the Exhibition was often criticized (most notably by the aesthete John Ruskin) for its display of High Victorian vulgarity. When the Exhibition closed on 11 October 1851 the building was dismantled and moved to Sydenham Hill. It opened to the public in 1854 and was popular with visitors until it burnt down in 1936. Commemoratives are very varied and range from chocolate boxes embossed with prints of the building to pottery and bone china produced in vast amounts. The more unusual items are the most valuable; photographs, glass and small useful wares are also very collectable.

▲ This plate is typical of a vast range of plates made to mark the Exhibition. The rococo-style border features various royal palaces. Other examples exist printed in purple, with vignettes in the border decoration embodying agriculture, commerce and the arts. The quality of the print will determine the value.

£100-150

▼ Potters continued to reproduce images of Crystal Palace after its move to Sydenham. This mug from c.1905 is a typical example of the seaside wares made to order from Germany. The hand enamelled print shows the Palace in its new elevation . The piece is less valuable than those made at the time of the Exhibition, but it is still collectable.

£30-50

◄ Although this jug by the Staffordshire firm of Cork, Edge and Malkin is of high quality the tree is a little too prominent and cuts the picture in half. The piece would have been accompanied by a basin. The unusual handle is in the form of harp – further musical motifs have been incorporated into the border.

£200-300

▲ Views of the Crystal Palace were reproduced in every form. The international figures on this vase show the worldwide appeal of the Exhibition. Reserves are decorated in simulated marble. **£80-120**

▼ The fine quality of this pot lid showing the "Grand International Building" is evident in the close detailing of the transfer print. The subject is relatively simple – lids with oak leaves or acorns would be more valuable. This lid was made by T. J. and J. Mayer who used the same polychrome method of decoration as F. & R. Pratt and Co. **£50-100**

◄ This lid features the opening ceremony of the Exhibition. A popular story tells how an unknown Chinese man who entered the Palace was allowed by Queen Victoria to stay, but was later found to be an intruder. The opening is a more common subject than the closing of the Exhibition – this lid is worth £100-150, but lids that show the closing are worth £700-1000.

POT LIDS

Decorative earthenware lids covering containers of toilet preparations and preserves were very popular during the Victorian period. The majority were made by F. & R. Pratt and Co., who decorated their wares in underglaze with polychrome transfer-printed engravings – often executed by Jesse Austin. Pratt lids can be distinguished from those by other makers by two small dots, usually in the "9 o'clock" and "3 o'clock" position, used for locating the transfer. Lids that still have their original container command a premium. Gilded borders are desirable but collectors should familiarize themselves with the types of gilding used at the time as sometimes the gilding has been applied later to make the piece seem more valuable. Lids continued to be popular until the 1880s. Modern reproductions are now being made, but these can be identified by the earthenware body, which is harder than that of the originals.

Albert's Death
(1861)

Prince Albert died of consumption at Windsor sanatorium on 14 December 1861 with Victoria holding his hand. The Queen, overcome with grief, never emerged completely from her mourning and retired from public life for over 25 years, only reappearing in 1887. The Prince had gained the country's respect, particularly after his involvement in the highly successful Great Exhibition, and on his death his memory was honoured by the Albert Memorial in Kensington Gardens which shows the Prince holding a catalogue of the Exhibition. The country went into a period of mourning and the Victorian age became known for its obsession with death. A vast range of funeralia was produced; several poets wrote lamentations, and potters produced a mass of commemoratives, many of which are of poor quality.

▼ This sombre print was reproduced on a number of different items, although any pieces found today are quite rare. The poignant composition shows Britannia holding a profile portrait medallion of Albert, standing beside a glum-faced lion. In the background is a view of the building for the 1862 exhibition the Prince never saw completed. The plate on the right has a basket weave border. The crack and relatively poor quality of the piece lower its value to around £150. The plate on the left, printed in more attractive sepia tones and with a more decorative moulded border, is undamaged and is more likely to fetch nearer £200.

£150-200 each

▼ Copeland & Garrett produced some of the first parian busts. This example of Victoria was made by them as one of a pair with Prince Albert in 1864, shortly after his death. The sculptor was William Theed who was commissioned to make the

busts by the Art Union of London. The crown of oak leaves identify it as a memorial piece.

£300-650

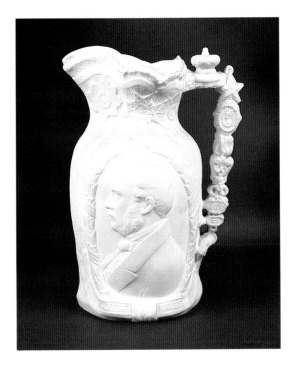

▼ One of the most inexpensive areas for the collector is that of printed ephemera. Pierced and embossed cards with a central lamentation were made by a number of "fancy stationers". Early ones such as this were usually highly elaborate and designed to be mounted on the wall. £80-100

▲ The dry-bodied stoneware of this jug is very similar to pari-an ware. The unglazed vitreous material is made non-porous, hard and dense by firing at a high temperature, which makes it ideal for moulding; the result is always remarkably crisp and fine. Sometimes the moulded decoration is edged in blue enamelling. This jug is one of the most common items for Albert's death and although it is very inventive it is not one of the most sought-after.

£200-300

► This plate bears a naive image of Albert. It would have been very inexpensive at the time but because it is now very rare it is a valuable collector's item.

£200-300

▲ One of the finest pieces commemorating the death of Prince Albert is this tazza by Copeland made two years after his death in 1863. It celebrates the Prince as promoter of the arts, champion of the universe and president of the society for science.

£700-900

The Golden Jubilee
(1887)

Royal coronations, jubilees and marriages had always been celebrated in style, but the 50th anniversary of the accession of Queen Victoria inspired unprecedented pageantry. The Golden Jubilee was to a large extent a political exercise. Victoria had gone into mourning following her husband's death in 1861, living as a recluse at Osborne house on the Isle of Wight, and the country needed something to restore their confidence in the Queen. Hence, the day was declared a national holiday. The new-fangled railway, a cheap and speedy alternative to the stagecoach, ferried revellers from all over England to London to see their beloved Queen ride through the streets and to attend a Thanksgiving service in her honour. Unlike previous jubilees, this one was shared by millions throughout the British Empire, and representatives were sent from India, Canada and all over the Colonies and the Dominions. For collectors, the 1887 jubilee is more popular than the diamond jubilee, partly because it was ten years earlier and partly because much of the commemorative material was of a type on offer for the first time. Most was made in England, and a lot of it was cheap and cheerful. Ceramics are particularly popular, and those of Doulton and Minton are most desirable.

▼ These plates were made by a Scottish potter in 1887. Collectors should beware being offered the first plate as a single item falsely commemorating the start of the reign. These designs were transfer-printed, but other examples are hand-coloured. Prices of plates depends on the rarity so collectors should familiarize themselves with the range. The fact that these plates are from Scotland increases their value.

£100-120 a pair

▲ Many mugs were made for the event. Most were fairly restrained (bottom) out of respect for the Queen's continued mourning, some were commissioned by the mayors of the towns as gifts to be presented at Sunday schools (centre), and others were produced to private commission (top).

£30-50

◀ Many octagonal plates were made at this time, with over 20 different printed designs. This one, made by Wallis Gimson who made a whole series of octagonal plates, is referred to as "the Balance of Payments Plate" as it bears the totals of imports and exports. The coloured hand-enamelling makes it more interesting, as many pieces at this time were in a single colour.

£150-250

▲ Even the most mundane objects were decorated with the Queen's image for her golden jubilee. This box was made to hold sewing cottons. The varnished print is in good condition.

£50-70

▶ Many pressed glass wares were made during Victoria's reign, mainly in northeast England, possibly by Sowerby or Davidson. This sugar bowl and jug are unusual and more desirable than most, being in amber rather than clear glass.

dish £80, jug £35-45

▲ The sepia transfer on this jardinière made for Victoria's jubilee shows the Queen flanked by the flags of India, Canada and Australia, in celebration of the strength of the British Empire. It is one of the largest ceramic commemoratives produced, and although unsigned is still highly desirable.

£1,000

◀ This teapot was made at the Hill Pottery for Burgess & Leigh. The shape is reminiscent of earlier Georgian forms. Teapots are particularly desirable, but are very vulnerable to damage so look for pieces that are in good condition.

£150-200

The Silver Wedding of the Prince and Princess of Wales
(1888)

The enthusiasm with which the marriage of the Prince of Wales to Princess Alexandra had been greeted in 1863 was repeated for their silver anniversary in 1888. Despite the Queen's hopes that marriage would force her wayward son to behave in a way more befitting his role as heir to the throne, the Prince of Wales continued with his often overt infidelities and gambling. Princess Alexandra treated her husband's lapses with great tolerance and humour, and by the time of the couple's anniversary had become a highly popular figure.

▲ This rare plate bears no inscription to say it is celebrating the anniversary of the Prince and Princess of Wales but the similarity of the print to that of other commemoratives at the time and the Prince of Wales's feathers suggest it was. The colours have been hand-enamelled onto the print – evident in the way they slightly overlap the edges.

£200-300

▼ The Prince of Wales was friendly with Henry Doulton whose firm made a number of commemoratives for the Prince. The pottery produced a whole range of commemoratives which even though mass-produced, were of very high quality. It began by making salt glazed stonewares, mainly for industrial purposes, and later adapted its techniques to produce domestic stonewares. This tyg follows a traditional design and colour scheme first used in the 18th century. On the reverse are the

moulded portraits of the Prince and Princess of Wales. The piece would be sought-after both by collectors of Doulton and of royal commemoratives.

£500

◄ The distinctive circular shape of this jug, the white porcelain, bright gilding and type of printing used, all indicate it was made in Germany for export to England. The poor quality of the portraits lowers the value.

£80-120

The Marriage of the Duke of York and Princess Mary
(1893)

Queen Victoria witnessed the marriage of her grandson (later George V) to Princess Mary of Teck. The Duke was the second son of the Prince of Wales and Alexandra. The Queen had originally selected Mary (or May, as she was known) as a partner for the Duke's older brother, Albert Victor (or Eddy), and they became engaged. Unfortunately he died of pneumonia in 1892, shortly before their planned wedding, and May married his brother a year later. Perhaps because of Eddy's death, commemoratives to celebrate the couple's marriage are not as prolific as those for their coronation in 1911, and those that do exist are highly collectable. Most pieces are made from pottery or porcelain, are unmarked, and follow the patterns established by the wares produced for Queen Victoria's golden jubilee (see pp. 74-5).

► This egg cup is a good example of the most basic commemoratives made. The naivety of the print has a charm which, together with the rare subject, make it highly collectable.

£30-50

▼ This home-made cushion in the form of the Victoria cross features a Stevengraph portrait of the Duke of York. Probably made as a love token, it includes panels of verse and religious motifs enclosed by glass-headed pins of turquoise, white and gilt metal. The anchor and battleships in the central panel refer to the Duke's naval background. It is a good example of the variety of ways in which royal images could be used.

£80-120

◄ This good quality cup and saucer with a finely transfer-printed and hand enamelled design was made by William Lowe of Longton, a sought-after maker. The gilding is still bright, suggesting the set has hardly been used. A mug exists with the same design. Sets are more valuable than single items. **£265**

The Crimean War
(1854)

Britain and France sent their troops to war with the Russians in the Crimea on 28 March 1854. Key battles were at Alma, Balaclava (scene of the Charge of the Light Brigade), Inkerman and Sebastopol. It fuelled great patriotism in the British who saw the Russians as a threat to the Empire, but popularity waned when accounts came back to Britain of the death toll. A declaration of peace was finally signed in Paris on March 30 1856. Staffordshire flatbacks, pot lids, woven silk pictures and Stevengraphs were all produced in large numbers to mark the event.

▲ This silkwork picture is woven with the figures of a Scottish highlander and a French infantryman. Its shape and size suggest it was a bookmark. Continued use has made it slightly faded – the colours would originally have been much brighter.

£80-100

◄ Portrait figures made to commemorate the Crimean War are the most collectable of all Staffordshire military figures. This example, entitled *The Victory*, shows a Frenchman, Englishman and a Turk, the three main allies involved in the war.

£1,000-2,000

▼ The well-known Staffordshire manufacturer Samuel Alcock produced this jug for the Royal Patriotic Fund. The print expresses the horror of the War rather than glorifying it – a weeping family is shown on one side, and the war wounded on the other. The quality of the print and the detailed decoration is of a very high standard. Although these jugs were produced in quite large quantities, those in good condition, such as this example, will command a high price.

£150-200

The Sudan

The Indian Mutiny was not commemorated, but later conflicts in the Sudan were. These centered around British attempts to suppress the Arabian slave trade in the 1860s and '70s. In 1879 the Zulu War was fought; the British arrived in Zululand to protect the Boers in January but, ill-prepared for the strength of the Zulus, were massacared. Further military defeats followed before Sir Garnet Wolseley defeated the Zulus on 4 July. The event is recorded on a jug printed with a bust of Sir Garnet, but few other items were made for this new embarrassment.

◀ General Charles Gordon (1833-85) put down the Taiping Rebellion in China in 1860 and earned himself the title of "Chinese Gordon" that appears on the back of this Doulton jug made for his death. He was governor of the Sudan from 1874 to 1879 during which time he abolished much of the slave trade. He was killed by the Mahdi at Khartoum whilst trying to maintain the defence of the city.

£120-180

◀ One of a series of hexagonal commemorative plates made by Wallis Gimson in Staffordshire, this example records Sir Henry Morton Stanley's arrival in Africa with a relief expedition to rescue Emin Pasha from the Mahdi in 1885. Dr Emin Pasha (or Emin Bey) was a physician who served under Gordon in the Sudan as a medical officer before succeeding him as governor of the Equatorial Provinces in 1878.

£80-120

▲ This very rare Doulton jug commemorates Stanley's expedition to relieve Emin Pasha. Stanley, an avid explorer, is best-known for his exploits in Africa where he found the missing explorer Dr Livingstone and uttered the now famous words "Dr Livingstone I presume?"

£200

The Boer War
(1899-1902)

The Boer War was fought without Victoria's full approval. However, Britain was at its height as an Empire and gun boat diplomacy was seen as an everyday solution to conflict. Britain had been gaining an increasingly strong hold on South Africa, including many States already under the occupation of the Boers (white residents of Dutch, German and Huguenot descent). The Boers became more and more enraged with colonial policy and on October 12 1899 war broke out. The Boers made impressive victories at first, but under Lord Roberts and Lord Kitchener Britain soon recovered, resorting to rather ruthless tactics and guerilla warfare.

▼ The style of this plate and the black transfer printed design suggest it is of German manufacture, although it was probably commissioned by a British retailer for export. The bright liquid gold decoration dates it to c.1900. Battle scenes were frequently depicted on Boer War commemoratives – another similar plate features a guardsman, a sailor and a colonel on land, perhaps to show the Navy's transferral of troops from sea to land battles in the Boer war.

£80-100

▲ One of the most sought-after commemoratives from the Boer War is this Copeland "subscriber's copy" loving cup. The colourful transfer printed and hand enamelled design includes a list of British victories and their dates. Initially the Boers made impressive victories as their forces were significantly larger than the British. However, when Lord Roberts was sent out as Commander-in-Chief with Lord Kitchener as his Chief-of-Staff, Britain soon recovered, resorting to guerrilla warfare and imprisoning thousands of women and children in concentration camps where many died. This piece bears the printed marks of Copeland and the retailers, T. Goode & Co.

£500-600

▲ Robert Baden-Powell (1857-1941) played an important part in the British victory in the Boer War. He is famed for having defended Mafeking from the Boers for seven months (1899-1900) – the subject of this Staffordshire mug. He later went on to greater fame when he founded the Boy Scouts in 1907.

£30-40

▲ Even the most humble wares commemorate the Boer War. These pin trays bear the words "A Souvenir of South Africa", a rather unusual phrase for a war commemorative.

£30-40 each

▼ For the Boer War British troops resorted to guerrilla warfare, abandoning their scarlet tunics for the khaki uniform more suited to the South African terrain. This Aller Vale jug records this departure with its portrait of a gentleman in khaki who appears on many wares.

£50

► Spelter was very popular during the last quarter of the 19th century in Britain and throughout Europe. This spelter portrait bust of Kitchener is one of several portraits of important military commanders. Spelter is a zinc alloy patinated to resemble bronze, but much cheaper to produce. However, it does suffer from surface oxidization which can produce unsightly bubbles (known as spelter disease). Also, when scratched the underneath shows as silver; on bronze pieces the underneath shows as a brassy colour.

£800-1,000

The Diamond Jubilee
(1897)

Britain and the Empire greeted the diamond jubilee of Queen Victoria's reign with even more gusto than they had her golden jubilee ten years earlier, and as with that jubilee, the day was declared a national holiday. The Empire was at its zenith and the British economy was flourishing. Many of the people celebrating her reign had been born within her lifetime and most felt a particular affection for the Queen. Every possible item was produced for the jubilee and nothing was considered too humble to be adorned with patriotic decoration – for example, chocolate boxes frequently bore the Queen's photograph. However, ceramics were still the most popular, often featuring vignettes of the royal palaces and royal family. Other items include colour prints, glassware and metalwork. Since the golden jubilee ten years earlier, colour printing had improved considerably and a number of diamond jubilee commemoratives bear witness to this. Some jubilee pieces were made to be sold exclusively in pairs, one bearing the coronation date and the other the date of the jubilee. It is important that these items are not separated and the one with the earlier date bought as a coronation piece.

▼ A number of mugs were made in enamel rather than ceramic. This beaker is decorated with the young Queen of 1837 on one side and the older Queen of 1897 on the other.

£50

▼ Wall plaques were popular throughout Victoria's reign. The colourful print on this Staffordshire example is not of very high quality and the value will be relatively low.

£50-80

▲ Royal commemoratives by the premier factories always command a premium – this two-handled loving cup for the Queen's diamond jubilee was made by Derby. The fine quality printing and gilding, together with the good condition of the piece add to its collectability.

£400-600

► Karel Nekola, the chief decorator at Robert Heron and Sons' Fife factory in Scotland, produced a range of Wemyss wares. This collectable range includes royal commemoratives covering the period from Queen Victoria's diamond jubilee to George V's coronation. Typically for such wares, the decoration on this Wemyss goblet is concentrated in the painted areas and the background is white. The sprays of cabbage roses and thistles are popular motifs.

£400

◄ By the end of Queen Victoria's reign smoking had become a popular pastime. Cigarette manufacturers put decorative cards in the packets which could be collected to make a complete set. These provide an affordable and exciting collecting area. This card is one of a set celebrating Victoria's reign.

£40-50

▲ The popular well-balanced design on this mug shows the Queen at three stages of her reign.

£100

◄ Britain was the largest producer of ceramic tiles in the world. The Staffordshire potters, Maw & Co., who made this tile, had a massive output. Many tiles were adapted as teapot stands, or were mounted and put on the wall; others were used to decorate fireplace surrounds.

£100

▲ The prints of the royal palaces on this Staffordshire Empire plate are typically colourful, in contrast to the single-coloured prints of the earlier jubilee.

£40-60

Personalities

A host of politicians and celebrities were featured in a variety of ways during the Victorian period, most frequently on ceramics. Parian was popular because it was less expensive than the white marble used in previous years, and enabled characters to be reproduced on a smaller scale. Staffordshire figures, affordable even for the working classes, were produced in abundance. Relief-moulded jugs depicted people including the poet Lord Byron and novelist Sir Walter Scott. Sportsmen were popular, particularly the early cricketers and rugby players. Fred Archer, the jockey, was one of several sports celebrities to appear on Stevengraphs as well as ceramics. Oher personalities regularly featured on items were Amelia Bloomer, Florence Nightingale and Dick Turpin.

► These amusing and appealing figures of Disraeli and Gladstone bear the impressed mark of W. S. and S. on the base, possibly for William Schiller & Son of Austria.

£80 each

► Queen Victoria heard the Swedish singer Jenny Lind (1820-87) when she came on tour to Britain in 1847. Known as the Swedish nightingale, Lind was portrayed by a number of leading British potters, including Minton and Wedgwood. She was also the subject of several caricatures, including an example of her as a candle snuffer with a bird's head and a woman's body. This Copeland parian bust was one of the first examples of her and is relatively rare.

£80-120

▼ These plates featuring Disraeli and Gladstone were made by Wallis Gimson and Co., as part of a series which includes the Prince of Wales (worth ten times more). The design, transfer-printed and

hand coloured, usually featured the celebrity with a list of his achievements. The firm used a beehive trademark on its plates.

£30-50 each

▲ Many Victorian potters made novelty wares. These teapots are part of a range dating from c.1900. Each one follows a similar style, but each lid represents a different personality.

£400-500

▲ Jewelry mourning the deaths of celebrities is rare. This jet brooch was made for Disraeli's death in 1881.

£100

▲ This children's plate was made for the death of Sir Robert Peel, the popular Conservative statesman, best known for his repeal of the Corn Laws in 1846.

£200

▼ This Staffordshire figural group represents the famous pugilists Heenan and Sayers. It has been reproduced during the past 20 years so collectors should be wary of excessive crazing, exceptionally bright gilding, a coppery tint and a lack of facial detail which appear on later copies.

£300-400

IMPORTANT PRIME MINISTERS

William Ewart Gladstone (1809-98) was Liberal Prime Minister between 1868 and 1874, between 1880 and 1885, in 1886, and again between 1892 and 1894. Among his achievements while in office were the passing of the education act in 1870, the disestablishment of the Church of Ireland and the carrying of a parliamentary reform act. Benjamin Disraeli (1804-81) was Gladstone's rival and helped to form modern Conservatism in England. He was Prime Minister in 1868 and again between 1874 and 1880, when he arranged the purchase of shares in the Suez canal. He was also a novelist – *Coningsby* and *Sibyl* both addressed social issues.

Death
(1901)

Queen Victoria died on 22 January 1901 at Osborne House at the age of 82, attended by members of her family and by her doctor of 20 years, Sir James Reid. She was Britain's longest serving monarch (64 years) – the majority of her subjects had not known another during their lifetimes. The Queen had made detailed instructions for her death and burial, which included having her hair cut and put into lockets, and having various articles buried with her in her coffin (many of them belonging to her late husband, but also a photograph of her loyal personal attendant John Brown, placed in her left hand). As requested, she was buried beside her husband Albert at Frogmore and people from all over the Empire came to mourn her. It was the first funeral of a monarch to be recorded on cinefilm, providing an opportunity for the Empire to be shown united in mourning. It is a sad irony that although the Victorian age was a period of obsessive interest in death, by the time of the Queen's death the fascination was beginning to wane, and relatively few memorial pieces were made for her. Many items take designs from wares made to celebrate the Queen's silver and golden jubilees.

▲ This colour print of Queen Victoria dates from the time of her diamond jubilee in 1897. It was re-issued for her death with the words "In memoriam of our beloved Queen Victoria" and given away with copies of the lady's magazine, *The Gentlewoman*.

£30-40

◀ An identical print to the one found on this memorial plate, but in colour, appears on a plate to celebrate the Queen's diamond jubilee (see p. 83). Black printing was frequently used for memorial wares. It is very unusual to find the name of the retailer – in this case, F Poulton of Reading – on the front of a piece, as it is usually printed on the back.

£80-100

◀ A wide range of printed ephemera was produced for Victoria's death. Although a still growing collecting area, mourning paraphernalia for the royal family commands a premium. This set comprises an announcement of Queen Victoria's death and black-edged royal stationery **£60-80**

▲ ▼ The aged look of this Staffordshire plate suggests poor quality production and the use of a porous material. The two holes at the top are for the ribbons that would have held it. The colour print and the gold dust border were fashionable at the time. The damage to the print – there is a tear across the Queen's body – will lower the plate's value. The print was popular in the final years of Victoria's life and appears on a number of other wares including this jug in the same style.

plate £45, jug £35

▶ The official form for the Queen's memorial service was distributed throughout the country and published in prayer books. Abundant at the time, the books are very rare today. This example, produced for Berwick-on-Tweed, is typical.

£25

▲ This card is important for any collector of royal ephemera. It has been suitably framed in ebony and set against a purple mount.

£50-70

▶ Among the more obscure collectables from Victoria's death is this felt scrap from the pavilion at Victoria Station on which her coffin was placed, together with remnants of the wreaths that decorated it and a letter of authenticity.

£40-60

Edward VII
(1901-1910)

The birth of Queen Victoria's son Albert Edward so soon after the birth of her first child (also Victoria) was not welcomed and led to a stormy relationship between mother and son that followed a pattern set by the three Georges and their sons. Edward had an unhappy childhood, cut off from contact with other children and subjected to the severe Teutonic discipline of his father, Albert. His mother did not trust him and denied him any involvement in government affairs. Not particularly scholarly, he devoted his time to good living – he enjoyed fine wine, food and women and travelled extensively, making trips to Canada and India and spending much of his time in France where he loved the colourful nightlife. In 1863 he married Princess Alexandra of Denmark with whom he had six children, but although he was happily married he continued to seek satisfaction elsewhere for his strong sexual appetite. When his mother died in 1901, the country feared that Edward was ill-prepared to be a competent ruler of the country, but he proved them wrong and was soon greatly respected. Coming to the throne at the late age of 60, he had calmed down a little and his latter-day pursuits concentrated on hunting and fishing at his country residence at Sandringham.

Edward's VII's greatest achievement during his reign was the securing of the Entente Cordiale between England and France in 1904, which earned him the title of Edward the Peacemaker; many pieces made for the King's death in 1910 bear this inscription. Also, in the first few months of Edward's reign, the Boer War came to an end, and occasionally the war is recorded on the wares made for his coronation. Items made for Edward's coronation are particularly interesting to the collector because they may bear one of two dates. The King contracted appendicitis shortly before the date originally set for the coronation, on 26 June 1902, and the day had to be

postponed to 9 August of that year. Commemoratives had already been made for the first date and because there was insufficient time to make new ones (and it would have been a costly and impractical exercise) most kept the original date. Consequently, any which bear the correct coronation date are rare and very collectable. As with previous monarchs, pottery and ceramics still dominated commemoratives. However, parian ware was declining in popularity and Staffordshire figures were being made in far fewer quantities than during the reign of Victoria. By this time polychrome colour printing had become commonplace on ceramics and many items for Edward's coronation and death bear portraits of the King and Queen surrounded by colourful flags and emblems. Generally, the wares from Edward's reign lack variety, and few innovative pieces were made at all. Some retailers, such as Harrods and Liberty's, still commissioned items, and the firm of Thomas Goode produced limited, deluxe and special Subscriber's editions, and these are among the most collectable commemorative items available today.

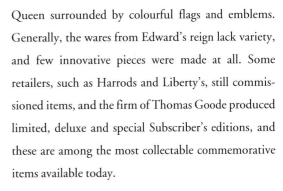

Left: A majolica jug depicting a portrait of King Edward VII encircled within a horseshoe border.

Above: A printed earthenware plate produced for the coronation of Edward VII in 1901.

The Coronation Postponed
(1902)

Like George IV, Edward spent a long time as the Prince of Wales before becoming King, and during his apprenticeship he led rather a wild and unconventional life. His mother, Queen Victoria, was frequently angered by his lifestyle and it was therefore a relief to her when the Prince married Alexandra, Princess of Denmark. The Prince ascended the throne in 1901 and his coronation was set for 26 June 1902, but he contracted appendicitis shortly before and the date was postponed to 9 August. Unfortunately commemoratives had already been produced bearing the earlier date, and consequently any wares with the later date are rare and at a premium (about 90% show the earlier date). Pieces were generally mass-produced and ceramics were usually transfer-printed, so it is important to look for quality of printing and good likenesses of the King in any decoration. Bone china tends to be more desirable than pottery. The Danish pottery, Royal Copenhagen, produced a number of commemoratives, in deference to the King's Danish wife. Other collectables from the coronation include horse brasses, handkerchiefs, Stevengraphs, beaded glassware, miniatures and militaria.

▲ William Moorcroft (1872-1945) was head of the Art Pottery department at Macintyre & Co. in Staffordshire, where he developed inventive forms and original designs. This mug credits the design to Arthur Lasenby Liberty who commissioned many of the pottery's wares. These mugs were given away by Mr and Mrs Liberty to friends and locals.

£150-200

▼ Hundreds of commemoratives were commissioned by the majors and aldermans of the various towns in Britain to be presented as gifts at coronation parties. Trivets, used as stands for teapots, were probably given to adults – children were usually given mugs.

£40-50

◄ A large number of plates were made by the premier potteries to celebrate the King's coronation, many with the King's head alone, others also with that of Queen Alexandra. On the base of this bone china Wedgwood plate is an inscription acknowledging the King's achievements. Similar plates were produced by Coalport in deluxe and less expensive versions.

£100-150

▲ It is obvious from the strong intensity of the August date on this beaker made for the town of Woking that it was added later.

£50-60

▲ Doulton made a number of bone china beakers for Edward's coronation. Some, like this example, bear only the year, fortuitously making them suitable for both dates. The piece has been covered in a primrose glaze and is finely gilded below the rim with an ornate band of stylized and trailing flower heads.

£100-150

▲ Printed ephemera from the King's coronation is highly collectable. This official programme was for the coronation that never took place. Usually programmes were thrown away so any examples found today are very rare. £30-40

◀ The production of Parian ware figures had rapidly declined by 1901; this figure of Edward in his coronation robes is one of the last examples. The maker is unknown, but the blue/grey hue of the porcelain and the quality of the moulding suggest the piece is continental.

£70-90

▼ Staffordshire flatback figures were experiencing a decline by the time of Edward's coronation. The enamels on this example are unstable (particularly evident in the black on the trousers) and the modelling is stiff. There has been no attempt to colour the King's beard and his cheeks are excessively red. Originally, the moulded base would have been highlighted in liquid gold, but this has worn off.

£50-80

The Death of Edward VII

Edward VII died on 6 May 1910, ending his short reign as British king. Although he had lived an extravagant life, he also had a strong interest in foreign policy; he played a leading part in maintaining peace in Europe, including instigating the signing of the Anglo-French peace treaty in 1904. His reign also coincided with peace in the Boer War (1 June 1901) and this earned him the name of "Peacemaker", a title which frequently appears on his funeral wares. The King was popular with his subjects and his death was greatly mourned, but there are significantly fewer commemoratives for his death than for his coronation.

▲ **Ridgway** produced a series of plates depicting views, and personalities such as Charles Dickens and William Shakespeare. This example has a photographic portrait of the late King. The whole has been covered with a treacle brown monochrome glaze which adds to the funereal feel, and the rim has been edged in gilt. Because the plate is in very good condition its value is higher than usual.

£50-70

▶ **Based in Burslem in Staffordshire, the firm of Booths Ltd** produced a number of earthenwares, many of which were copies of early Worcester porcelain. Although there is no reference to the King's death on this Booths' plate, it is obviously a memorial piece as the King's portrait is surmounted by that of his brother and successor to the throne, George V, and his Queen, Mary of Teck. Other vignettes show scenes from the Channel Islands. It is unusual and desirable to find a piece bearing the portrait of the two monarchs.

£50-80

▼ **Wall plaques** are less common than wall plates and when well-decorated command a premium. This plate has a flow blue glaze – a deep cobalt colour with a hazy outline that was unintential but proved popular in the 19th century. The striking image of the King and the moulded border all add to the value.

£50-80

► This prayer book is very rare and has survived in good condition, but like other religious books, would not command a particularly high price. It contains the funeral service of the King at the front and an ordinary prayer and hymn book at the back. The cover is of gilt tooled leather. The inscription inside refers to the King as "King Edward the Peacemaker". The laurel border around the King's portrait is in purple, a typically funereal colour.

£20-30

▲ The King is often depicted in full military uniform of scarlet tunic and pale blue sash bedecked with medals. This large pottery rectangular dish is particularly decorative. The border, moulded into the shape of acanthus leaves, has four panels transfer printed with rose sprigs and a rim highlighted in gold.

£40-50

▼ This fine porcelain vase was commissioned by Thomas Goode from Copeland-Spode to commemorate Edward's death and was issued in different editions with varying degrees of gilding. £500-700

AT THE FRONT!

Every fit Briton should join our brave men at the Front.

ENLIST NOW.

George V
(1910 - 1936)

The eldest son of Edward VII, Albert Victor the Duke of Clarence, died in 1892, leaving his brother, George, as heir to the throne. Like William IV, George had a naval background, which gave him a cheerful and appealing character. Through his fine leadership and commitment to his role as a constitutional monarch he earned a great affection for the monarchy among the working classes which continues today. His voice was the first of a monarch to be heard by the masses when his Christmas speech was broadcast to the nation; he further endeared himself when he revived the old tradition of personally distributing money to the poor every Maundy Thursday. George's reign was a time of global instability – the First World War began in 1914, home rule was given to Ireland in 1921, and in 1931 the

Statute of Westminster removed the government's direct power over the Commonwealth. Members of the Empire became restless – India, for example, placed increasing pressure on Britain for self rule. At home, women fought for greater equality and gained the right to vote in 1918; the first Labour Ministry was formed under Ramsay Macdonald in 1924; the trade unions led a General Strike in 1926; and an economic depression followed the Wall Street Crash of 1929.

George V's reign saw a massive ouptut in commemoratives, particularly ceramics, as Britain was now the "potter of the world". Shapes were often in the "Art Deco" style of the 1920s and items were far less elaborate than during Victoria's reign. Improvements in machines and methods of mass-production led to a wealth of low-cost colour-printed mugs, ornaments and tablewares, and more commemoratives were made for the King's coronation than ever before. Even more were produced for the Great War which was seen as an opportunity to spread jingoistic patriotism throughout Britain and the Empire. Most were made after hostilities had ended, as during the war all efforts were concentrated on fighting. The most poignant war collectables are the silk woven postcards

the troops sent back home. Also of interest are the cartoons of Bruce Bainsfather and the plethora of crested bone china souvenirs depicting war machines and battleships, made by Goss, Grafton, Arcadia and Savoy. Among the most decorative wares are the character jugs modelled by Carruthers Gould for Wilkinson and Co., brightly-coloured and in gilt; and a series of tiles produced by George Cartlidge bearing portraits of the military commanders and politicians of the day. The women's suffrage movement prompted a number of items, often satirical and titled, many made in Germany. George V was the first Emperor to visit the British Empire when he went to India with his wife in 1911 for the Delhi Durbar, and many wares from the early part of his reign reaffirm the power of the Empire. The King's Jubilee in 1935 saw the launch of the first official design by the British Pottery Manufacturers Federation, which continued to launch designs up to the Silver Jubilee of Elizabeth II. The King died in 1936 and although greatly mourned, very few pieces mark his death – probably the most famous is an earthenware two-handled cup by Doulton, entitled "A Royal Exemplar", which gives the fitting epitaph to the King as "The Friend of his People".

Left: An "At the Front" poster issued by The Parliamentary Recruitment Committee for the First World War, 1914.

Above: A Doulton limited edition loving cup produced for George V's silver jubilee, 1935.

The Coronation
(1910)

Although George was the second son of Edward VII, he inherited the throne in 1910, as his younger brother had died in 1892. He was crowned with his wife, Mary of Teck, a year later on 22 June, and they were both popular with their subjects. During the First World War they visited the front and their daughter, Princess Mary, supplied troops with cigarettes issued in gilt metal tins, just as Victoria had sent her troops boxes of chocolates during the Boer War. By the time of George's accession the pottery industry had become highly accomplished in the art of making commemoratives, using the latest techniques. Many coronation souvenirs were, and have remained, relatively inexpensive. The most desirable ceramics are those made by premier factories such as Doulton, Derby, Worcester, Wedgwood and Coalport, and those designed by Moorcroft for the Macintyre factory (Moorcroft's own factory did not open until 1913).

▲ The grey-white paste and bright gilding of these figural jugs (both have handles at the back) are typical of pieces made in Germany for export to Britain during the run-up to the coronation. Jugs of this type are nearly always marked "Made in Germany", sometimes within a circle.

£70-90

▼ Many potteries produced commemorative mugs decorated with colour prints of the King and Queen on one

side and left blank on the reverse, leaving room for special inscriptions to be inserted. This bone china mug was commissioned by Whitworth Council, but the same print can be found on mugs printed with the names of various other organizations.

£25-35

► This rather busy design is typical of commemoratives produced by William Lowe of Longton. The reverse bears Lowe's mark of the letter "WL" above an "L". The elephant in the design probably refers to India – in the year of the coronation King George V and Queen Mary visited Delhi and were crowned Emperor and Empress at the Durbar (public audience).

£80-100

◀ The biscuit-coloured body of this pair of Stafford-shire coronation portrait busts has possibly been used in a vague attempt to imitate Royal Worcester fig-ures. The bases are painted black to simulate the slate used on more expensive busts. Although very inex-pensive when first pro-duced these figures are collectable today. Their hand-painted lips and eyes are attractive details which add to their desirablity.

£80-100

LITHOPHANES

Among the novelties worth looking out for from George V's coronation are beakers with lithophanes incorporated into the base. Lithophanes are fine-quality plaques of biscuit porce-lain with moulded decoration which can be viewed only when held up to the light. They were first made in c.1830 but contin-ued in production through the early part of the 20th century. In the case of royal commemora-tives, the moulded decoration was usually a portrait of the reigning monarch. The German factories such as Berlin KPM made some particularly fine litohophanes, although Wedg-wood in Britain also produced some. The plaques were often incorporated into lanterns and lights and although quite popu-lar in the bottoms of tankards, they very rarely appear in cups and mugs. Lithophane beakers featuring Queen Mary are rarer and therefore more expensive than those with a portrait of King George.

▲ Harrods' exclusively designed beaker marked on the base with their name was sold only through their famous store. Although the quality of the beaker and colour print is high, the design itself is not particu-larly unusual or original.

£30-40

▲ Prayer books are among the more unusual objects made to mark the coronation. This leather bound one contains pho-tographs of the new monarchs, the coronation service and an ordinary prayer and hymn book.

£15-25

99

Emancipation

The movement for female emancipation had begun in the late 19th century, with a gradual increase in the numbers of women taking up professional positions, often against the wishes of male members of the same profession. Great progress was made in furthering the female cause when Emmeline and Christabel Pankhurst formed the Women's Social and Political Union in 1903. Their organization grew at a rapid rate, taking the government of the day by surprise. Members were passionate in their ideals, and many were arrested in the course of the ensuing campaign. During the First World War the essential work carried out by women greatly assisted their cause, and the bill permitting women to vote was finally passed in 1918. Among the most desirable but rare objects connected with the cause are sashes and rosettes worn during the campaigns.

◄ **Emmeline Pankhurst is modelled here from creamware and shown delivering her message with characteristic gusto. Creamware figures of this date are very rare; their golden age was pre-1820.**

£200-250

► **Novelty intarsio-ware teapots, such as this one depicting Mrs Pankhurst, were made by Wileman & Co, later to become Foley and in turn Shelley. This is one of the most sought after of their range, worth over twice as much as more readily available personalities such as Chamberlain (see p. 102).**

£1,000-1,500

► **This amusing but unflattering portrayal of a lady, made at the Royal Doulton factory at Burslem, typifies the often satirical interpretation of the female cause. The glazed stoneware figure takes the form of an inkwell and was modelled by Leslie Haradine, one of Royal Doulton's premier modellers of figures during the 1920s and '30s.**

£200

► **This group is made from bisque, an unglazed, tinted porcelain, popular for making dolls. It was probably made for export in Germany, the chief manufacturer of bisque figures and dolls at this time.**

£150-250

The Titanic

The Titanic sank on the night of 14 April 1912 whilst on its maiden voyage, after crashing into an iceberg in the North Atlantic off the Coast of Newfoundland. Among the 2,200 people on board, many of them celebrities, over 1,500 died. The ship, the most advanced of its day, was thought to be indestructible and research is still going on to try and ascertain the cause of the sinking. The disaster has inspired films and books and there has even been an auction specifically for Titanic memorabilia. The most common items to come up for sale are the telegrams sent from the rescue ship Carpathia by survivors to their loved ones at home. Also available are the texts of radio messages sent from the Titanic, photographs of the Captain and the ship and letters sent by passengers before the ship sank.

▼ **This Marconigram written by Captain Arthur Rostron of the *Carpathia* and sent by Harold Cottam, is informing New York of the *Titanic* disaster. It was one of a collection of more than 400 original signals with a total estimated value of over £30,000. Because the *Carpathia* was overloaded with private signals from the survivors, many of them had to be handwritten by the sender. Other collectable telegrams include messages sent before the disaster by the *Titanic*'s Captain, Edward Smith, and some 85 signals sent during the disaster, one of which reads "Sinking wants immediate assistance".**

▲ **These *Titanic* mourning postcards are typical of the mourning ephemera produced during the Victorian time. They bear a religious verse and a tragic picture in sepia, and are a foretaste of the cards and postcards made in quantity during the First World War. Other *Titanic* postcards that come up for sale are those made before the sinking which have been signed by survivors at a later date.**

£20-25 each

World War 1
(1914-18)

The Great War started in 1914, only three years after the accession of George V, and it was to bring about the deaths of more subjects than all the combined conflicts of Queen Victoria's 60-year reign. The war aroused patriotic fervour and anti-German sentiments, prompting George V to change his family name from Saxe-Coburg to Windsor. The Staffordshire potters produced numerous wares to show British solidarity. Most war items fall into two groups: those celebrating the British allegiance with France, Russia, Japan, Belgium and Italy (often featuring the flags or military leaders of each country); and those marking the Armistice of 1918 and peace of 1919. However the range was diverse. Models of tanks, zeppelins, ambulances and dugouts were made; colourful personalities were commemorated; recipients of the Victoria Cross were featured on matchboxes; and printed ephemera and silkwork postcards abounded.

▶ Some of the most impressive war items were the character jugs modelled by Carruthers Gould. These examples represent (left to right) Field Marshall Haig, President Wilson and Marshal Joffre. Value depends on the rarity of the particular figure.

£450-650 each

▲ This character teapot representing Joseph Chamberlain is one of a number of similar intarsio wares produced by the Foley factory (see also pp. 82 and 100).

£150-250

▼ This bone china teaplate inscribed "European War 1914" is typical of wares produced early on in the conflict to mark the outbreak of war.

£20-30

◀ The spiral fluted decoration on this Astbury beaker was a popular way of creating a simple, yet decorative effect; the flutes terminate in an attractive scalloped rim highlighted by gilding.

£25-35

▼ The *Lusitania* in this cut woolwork picture was sunk by a German U-boat on 7 May 1915 with the loss of some 1,200 lives, including 128 Americans. The event finally led to American intervention in the Great War. **£100-150**

▼ The superior quality of this Goss souvenir plate from the seaside resort of Barmouth is reflected in the standard of the print. The flags here have a realistically windswept appearance and they are arranged effectively to fill the rim of the plate.

£80-100

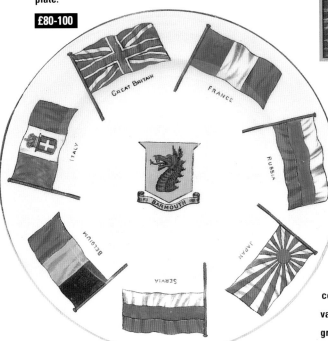

▼ "Take up the Sword of Justice", was one of the most potent recruiting posters, showing the figure of Justice surrounded by drowning figures and the sinking *Lusitania* n the horizon. The poster was

designed by Bernard Partridge (1861-1945), a stained glass artist who became a renowned political cartoonist and illustrator, working for *Punch* Magazine and other publications. As with any type of printed ephemera, condition is critical to value; tearing or foxing will greatly reduce the price.

£60-90

RECRUITING POSTERS

About 150 different poster designs were published during the First World War in a recruiting drive of unprecedented efficiency. Emotive slogans and images were designed to incite the youth of Britain to take up arms. The posters were published by the Parliamentary Recruiting Committee, which was formed at the beginning of the war under the jurisdiction of, among others, the Prime Minister Herbert Asquith. By 1916 the number of volunteers joining the armed forces had diminished to such an extent that conscription was introduced.

World War I – Peace

By the time representatives of the new republic of Germany signed an Armistice on 11 November 1918 over 10 million people had perished, nearly 750,000 of them members of British forces. Following the Armistice, the Peace Treaty of Versailles was agreed and signed on 18 June 1919.

In view of the tragically large loss of life it is not surprising that on wares made to mark the cessation of hostilities, the word "Peace" is featured more prominently than the word "Victory", which is usually highlighted. Whereas earlier First World War plates usually refer to "The European War", on later commemoratives, the scale of the conflict had prompted most potters to term it the "Great War". Most wares follow the pattern established by earlier commemoratives, using the flags of allies and portraits of military leaders, together with an inscription and the date of the Armistice.

▼ Tanks, battleships and planes – the implements of war – are incorporated into the design of this rather over-elaborate plate which also features portraits of Admiral Beatty, Field Marshall Haig and Lloyd George, surrounded by a biscuit-coloured border. The tank was invented during the First World War and commemoratives from this time feature some of the earliest representations of the vessel. This plate bears the word "Victory" rather than the more frequently used "Peace".

£50-70

▲ In this well-designed beaker, a transfer-printed sepia figure, emblematic of peace and victory, is shown holding the victor's laurel. The design is enlivened by the additonal hand-enamelling of the surrounding flags.

£25-35

▼ Although this transfer-printed cup celebrating peace is embellished with high-quality hand-enamelled decoration , its value would be considerably reduced because the gilding on the rim is badly worn.

£25-35

◀ This Staffordshire pottery mug bears portraits of Admiral Beatty who received the surrender of the German fleet in 1918; and Field Marshall Haig, who persuaded the supreme commander of the allied forces, Marshal Foch, to extend his attack north and so break the Hindenburg Line.

£30-40

▲ Many local authorities and co-operatives commissioned their own wares to celebrate the signing of the Peace Treaty in 1919 which signalled the end of the war. Although some designs were specially devised, more frequently they were adapted from pieces made for general production and further adorned with the name of the authority concerned.

£25-35

▼ The same pattern was often adapted by potters for different types of ware. Here the same print has been used on a beaker as on a mug. Although only slight, the variations between the two designs – the words "The Great World War" and the dates 1914 which feature on the mug have not been used on the beaker – make the mug more valuable.

Mug £30-40
Beaker £25-30

▼ David Lloyd George was a Welsh Liberal politician who became Prime Minister of a coalition government in 1916, and remained in power for the following

eight years (until 1922). This well-modelled jug, with attractive semi-translucent soft glazes dates from the later years of the war, or maybe from after the war. A similar jug of Lloyd George's predecessor, Asquith, was made by the same factory. **£100-150**

Home and Empire

The post-war years of George V's reign witnessed a fundamental alteration in the face of British society. The "roaring 20s" was a period of renewed hope and optimism and rapid change, and events such as the Empire Exhibition of 1924 provided reminders that Britain was still leader of an empire. But beneath the veneer of hope, political dissatisfaction simmered; rumblings in India resulted in confrontations and subsequent fatalities; by 1921 there were over 2 million unemployed and the 1926 General Strike was symptomatic of the disillusionment of many low-paid workers.

This was also an age of rapid technological advancement; the invention of the radio provided a common link for the nation; John Alcock and Arthur Whittam Brown crossed the Atlantic in an aeroplane for the first time in 1919; and the luxury liner *Queen Mary* provided the affluent classes with the ultimate way to travel in comfort and opulence.

◄ The Wembley lion was taken as the symbol for the Empire Exhibition held in 1924. It was one of the most important trade exhibitions of the decade and large numbers of ceramic wares, many made by Britain's premier factories, were among the numerous items produced to mark the event. This jasperware two-handled loving-cup, made by Wedgwood, is appropriately adorned with the Exhibition's Wembley lion motif.

▼ Interesting new designs evolved in the 1920s. Among the most innovative objects made for the Empire Exhibition is this novelty clock teapot made by Collingwood Harpers. When twisted the lid shows the time in different parts of the Empire.

£150-250

£40-60

◄ Scale models of this quality are keenly collected by both corporate and private collectors; this model is probably contemporary with the *Queen Mary*, the flagship of the Cunard line. The quality is obvious not only in the detail, but also in the expensive plinth on which the liner is mounted. **£5,000-7,000**

► Cricket was one game which brought together the various dominions of the Empire on the sports field. This 1930s Coalport plate featuring W. G. Grace, the pioneer of modern cricket, will appeal to collectors of cricket memorabilia and be keenly sought after.

£100-150

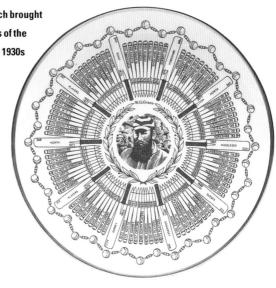

▲ The pride Britain took in the liner the *Queen Mary* is reflected in the very large number of diverse objects which were produced to celebrate its building between 1930 and 1934. This game, one of the more unusual *Queen Mary* commemoratives, was perhaps intended to give some idea of how difficult it is to steer such a large ship and may originally have been sold on board the liner.

£30-40

▼ The novelty of the radio can be gauged by the large numbers of objects in which this new method of communication features. A type of early radio, the crystal set, was worked by adjusting an instrument called "a cat's whisker". This cup and saucer from c.1930 shows young girls playing with their crystal set and is decorated on the rim with pictures of the receiving aerial and speaker horn.

£40-60

▼ Objects from the General Strike of 1926 are rare and keenly sought-after. This match holder is moulded in chalk and has then been hand-coloured.

£50-60

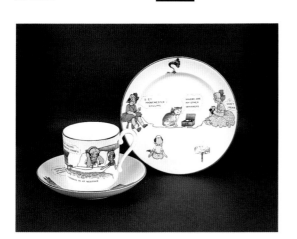

1935 Silver Jubilee

After the Armistice of 1918 the makers of commemoratives had to wait 17 years before another suitable event occurred on which they could capitalize to such a degree. By the time of the 1935 jubilee the map of Europe had been redrawn and further conflict seemed inevitable. But despite growing political unrest the monarchy retained the affection of the people and for many the jubilee provided a welcome diversion from the difficulties of everyday life.

The range of ceramic objects produced for the jubilee differed significantly from those made for earlier events. Designs became more adventurous, the geometric Art Deco style, now popular in "modern" households, took hold. Nonetheless, all too often innovative shapes were decorated with traditional printed designs similar to those used for the coronation 25 years earlier, and the now elderly couple look slightly incongruous set against such novel streamlined backgrounds.

▼ **Many enterprising manufacturers produced a wide range of inexpensive jubilee commemoratives. This sheet metal tray was made in India. It has been machine embossed with the name of the manufacturer and was probably intended for the colonial market.**

£30-50

▲ **The Star China Co. began producing commemoratives in 1911 stamped with the trade name Paragon, and by 1935 started making the distinctive fine-quality wares with which its name has become synonymous. This loving cup and mug are typically decorated with sepia portraits of the King and Queen within blue laurel frames. The handles are elaborately decorated with the rose, thistle and shamrock. Paragon made items to this design in different sizes and quality, so value varies considerably; loving cups are more expensive. The most valuable Paragon jubilee item is a large loving cup with lavishly gilded handles and a gilded inscription inside the rim.**

Loving Cup £120-180

Mug £60-90

▲ The decoration of this simple pottery mug made by Booths shows the juxtaposition of new and old which was typical of many jubilee pieces. It bears the formal portraits of the King and Queen framed within a traditional laurel wreath, but has a novel handle and is edged with a smart silver rim.

£35-50

▶ Among the more unusual jubilee objects are these candlesticks, which have been colour printed with double portraits of George and Mary and which were retailed by the Co-Op store. The candlesticks are especially unusual because they have retained their original packaging thus greatly increasing their desirability to collectors.

£40-50

▲ The shaded pink areas on this Crown Devon mug highlight the extent of the British Empire in 1935. The flared shape and triangular handle have a strong Art Deco feel.

£30-40

▲ **BEWARE**

This strange fake jubilee jug uses a shape that is quite wrong for the period. The jug is made from bone china colour printed with a portrait of the King and Queen in a suspiciously pale sepia. It is marked on the base with the same crown that appears above the date. Similar fakes have been made to celebrate Victoria's jubilee and the coronation of George VI.

▲ Although originally very inexpensive and produced in large numbers, tinplate wares such as this mug are nowadays relatively scarce. This one was commissioned by the local

authority of the town of Greenock and given to local school children. Because tinwares were very inexpensive when they were made, most of them have been subjected to very heavy wear and tear and this can affect value. Although this mug seems to have been well-used it has remained in reasonable condition.

£35-45

Family Life

Despite the political turmoil of his reign, George V enjoyed a relatively happy family life. He had six children, of whom his two eldest sons Edward and Albert appear most often on commemoratives. George conferred the Dukedom of York on his second son Albert (later George VI) in 1920, and was delighted with his marriage to Lady Elizabeth Bowes Lyons in 1923 and the births of the Princesses Elizabeth and Margaret Rose. Considering that neither Princess was directly in line to the throne, it is remarkable how many items were made for their births and childhood. George's relationship with his eldest son and heir Edward was to prove more problematic, although prior to his entanglement with Mrs Simpson, he earned the affection of the public through his visits to sites of inner city deprivation and his promises (although unfulfilled) of help to the Welsh miners in the depression years.

▲ The portrait of Edward, the Prince of Wales, featured on this bone china Doulton beaker is unusual because it shows him formally attired in a top hat and bow tie.

£50-60

◀ Only the inscription on the base of these Paragon tablewares, which reads "For HRH The Duchess of York for Princess Elizabeth" shows that they were made to commemorate the birth of the Princess in 1926. The attractive magpie design is believed to be a reference to the two birds which, according to popular legend, flew around the house at the time of Elizabeth's birth. The caption "two for joy" is an extract from a popular verse about magpies, which opens with the line "One for sorrow".

£50-70 (for set)

▼ The design on this Paragon set made for the birth of Princess Margaret is symbolic; the marguerites and roses represent the princess's name Margaret Rose. Other pieces include a coffee pot and a serving plate. **£50-70 (for set)**

▼ This tea caddy is one of the very few pieces made for the wedding of George, the Duke of Kent to Princess Marina in 1934, and it is therefore quite collectable. **£30-40**

▲ The enchanting photograph of Princess Elizabeth as a young child that appears on this dish was taken by the royal photographer Marcus Adams. The series was issued in 1928/9 by the Paragon factory. Commemoratives with good quality photographic portraits are always in demand but this particular example would be especially desirable as it is in pristine condition. **£40-60**

▼ This Princess Elizabeth doll was made in the late 1930s by the Chad Valley Co. Ltd, a leading British doll manufacturer. Chad was granted a Royal Warrant in 1938, after which time its labels read "Toy Makers to H.M. The Queen". This doll has a typically finely moulded felt face with glass eyes, mohair wig and stuffed velvet body. Condition is crucial, as dolls are vulnerable to moth damage which can be impossible to repair. **£80-120**

Royal Visits

With the exception of a trip to India in the year of their coronation, George V and Queen Mary's visits were limited to destinations within the British Isles. However, several other members of the royal family undertook extensive trips overseas. The Prince of Wales was the keenest traveller, visiting Canada, South Africa and Argentina; and the Duke and Duchess of York and the Duke of Gloucester made official visits to Australia in 1927 and 1934. Many of the objects made to commemorate royal visits were intended to be given as presents to local school children, or sold inexpensively through retail outlets. Ceramic wares, lapel badges, book marks, pencils and other small items were often inscribed with the place name and date of a visit for this purpose.

► Items made for George and Mary's trips are scarce, possibly because as they were only of local interest they were made in quite small numbers. This mug marks a visit to the Isle of Man. It has retained its gilt rim in near perfect condition and this will add to its value. **£50**

◄ This mug celebrating a royal trip to Frodsham in July 1925 is of unusually high quality – the majority of such pieces are far less refined.

The handsome, softly-coloured head and shoulders printed portrait shows George V wearing a ceremonial uniform.

£20-30

► This mug celebrates a trip made by the King and Queen to Stoke-on-Trent in 1913. It contains the maximum amount of information and decoration possible, featuring portraits of the King and Queen on one side, and on the other, the town arms together with a ribbon inscribed with the name of the mayor. **£25-35**

Death
(1936)

By 20 January 1936, the King lay gravely ill in a coma. To spare the feelings of his assembled family, and to ensure that the announcement of his death was printed in the morning papers rather than the evening journals, his death was hastened by the intervention of royal physician, Lord Dawson, who administered a lethal injection. The public was prepared for the King's death by Dawson's statement that "the life of the King is moving peacefully to its close". In his notebook Dawson vividly remembered how, with members of his family around him, the king died "... so quietly and gently that it was difficult to determine the actual moment." (The facts of George's death were only revealed in 1986, in Francis Watson's biography of Dawson.) Compared with wares made for the deaths of previous monarchs, few pieces were made to commemorate the death of George V and the Victorian preoccupation with death did not last into the 20th century.

▼ George V was the first monarch to address the nation on Christmas day by radio so this volume of his recorded speeches is very collectable. **£50-100**

▲ Perhaps the most strikingly simple and effective commemorative for George's death was this Doulton two-handled cup, decorated with a photographic portrait on a buff ground, and entitled against a white riband "Royal Exemplar", reversed with a similar ribbon titled "The Friend of his People".

£100-150

► Although George V memorial ceramics are few and far between, various other media were used to record his death, many of them reflecting the rapid technological advancements made during his reign. This Kodak film depicting the funeral procession would be sought-after not only for its historical appeal, but because it is in its original box and because it is of interest to collectors of early cine material.

£20-30

Edward VIII

(1936)

Edward VIII, the eldest son of George V, was educated at the Royal Naval College and then spent two years at Magdalen College in Oxford before serving with the Grenadier Guards in the First World War. On 13 July 1911 he was invested as Prince of Wales at Caernarvon Castle in Wales. He was a fine ambassador of his father, the King, and spent six years travelling the world on official tours between 1919 and 1925. He came to the throne on the death of his father in January 1936, and is most famous as "the King that was never crowned". His youth and good looks made him very popular, and he became a leader of fashion. Yet another royal *bon viveur*, his love of women, together with his lack of respect for royal protocol, led to his downfall. His much-publicized affair with the married Mrs Wallis

Simpson caused a government crisis and he was forced to abdicate on 11 December 1936, as it became clear to him that the King of England could not be married to a twice-divorced lady. Granted the title of His Royal Highness the Duke of Windsor by his brother George VI, he spent the rest of his years in self-imposed exile in France until his death from cancer in 1972.

Edward's coronation was planned to take place in May 1937 and the potters had greeted the event with their usual enthusiasm, so that by the time the King had abdicated most wares were already on the market. It is a mistaken belief that anything connected with Edward VIII is rare and collectable as he was king for only 11 months and his reign never culminated in a coronation. This is not true, as vast quantities of wares were made – rarest are the few coins issued by the Royal Mint.

As with commemoratives made for the reign of George V, most pottery wares made during the reign of Edward VIII were in the Art Deco style – the most interesting are those produced for Wedgwood by their chief designer, Keith Murray, which reflect the new "Modern" approach to design. Other Modernist prints came from Dame Laura Knight whose design for a mug – of the King's profile, St George and the Dragon and an elephant on one side, and the Royal Arms on the other – was reproduced in many sizes by a number of makers and was adapted for George VI commemoratives. Clarice Cliff, Eric Ravilious and the firm of Shelley also produced new and interesting designs.

However, there were some unfortunate mismatches, with tired old traditional prints applied somewhat incongruously to Art Deco shapes. Some musical mugs were made and these are very collectable. There was also a revival in the British glass-making industry at this time and a number of finely engraved commemoratives were produced by such companies as Webb, in the form of loving cups, wine glasses and tumblers, usually engraved with the royal cypher and sometimes enclosing metal medallion portraits of the King. The rarest pieces are those made to commemorate the abdication and these are highly collectable. Memorial wares are also rare, and only one of the top makers – Coalport – is known to have made anything to mark Edward's death in 1972 (a plate produced in a limited edition of 100). Few pieces were made bearing the portrait of Mrs Simpson, and these too are collectable.

Left: A utility teapot by Sadler for Edward VIII's coronation, 1937.
Above: An Edward VIII coronation medallion 1937.

The Proposed Coronation
(1937)

When George V died in 1936 he was suceeded by his eldest son, Edward Prince of Wales. Edward was, perhaps, better prepared for his role as Britain's future king than any of his predecessors. He had served in the Grenadier Guards during the First World War, had travelled extensively both abroad and in England, and was regarded as very much a man of the people – someone on whom the population of Britain could trust to understand their needs and problems. However, his decision in 1937 to marry Mrs Wallis Simpson, an American divorcee, led to a constitutional crisis and his abdication, in favour of his younger brother Albert, who was later crowned George VI. Wares made for the planned coronation of Edward VIII were all produced well before the event, thus a surprisingly large number of coronation pieces exist, even though the King was never crowned. Objects which particularly stand out are those designed by artists with a more modernist style than had previously been seen; among the most notable are tablewares by Eric Ravilious, Dame Laura Knight, and Keith Murray.

▲ Not all coronation commemoratives were of high quality. This teapot is a run-of-the-mill utility ware which has been adapted for the coronation. Although unisgned, it may have been made by Sadler, a prolific producer of brown earthenwares of this type.

£40-60

▼ This mug was designed by the celebrated artist Laura Knight and made by the Wilkinson factory. Knight's transfers were widely available and other potters made similar mugs. Wilkinson mugs came with certificates of authenticity which can double their value.

£80 (with certificate)

◄ This Wedgwood jasperware portrait medallion follows a tradition established by Josiah Wedgwood in the 18th century, when the factory made vast numbers of similar plaques depicting royal, aristocratic and political luminaries. However, the fact that the King is in informal contemporary dress shows some attempt at modernity.

£100-150

► This white character jug was made by the Derbyshire-based Bretby factory, which often added original touches to its designs. This jug has a handle in the form of an "E" and is decorated in a distinctive semi-matt glaze.

£60-80

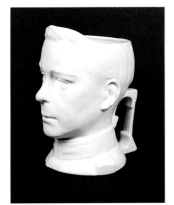

► One of the more unusual objects made for the coronation is this brass corkscrew. Few metal objects survive and although inexpensive, this would still be sought-after by collectors.

£20-30

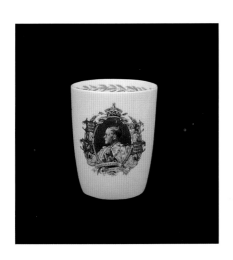

▲ Royal Doulton produced a wide variety of wares for the coronation, including this fairly standard quality beaker and mug with traditional decoration. Among the rarer Doulton pieces is a biscuit-coloured two-handled loving cup with a portrait of Edward surrounded by flags.

£60-80 (mug)

£50-60 (beaker)

◄ This bone china mug, made by the Windsor Pottery for the Co-operative Society, shows a compromise between modern and traditional styles. The handle is a novel innovation, but the portrait surrounded by banners and flowers harks back to traditional forms.

£120

Abdication and Death

The King announced his abdication in a radio broadcast to the nation on 11 December 1936, and departed for Europe soon afterwards. He became HRH Duke of Windsor, but as a measure of the disapproval of the royal family, after her marriage to the Duke in June 1937, Wallis Simpson was only allowed the title of Royal Duchess, not Royal Highness. The couple spent most of their life in exile in France. The fact that his mother never forgave him for his marriage was the cause of lasting pain to the Duke. His valet who tended him at his death in France in 1972 recorded that his last words were "Mama, Mama, Mama, Mama". The Duchess died 14 years after the Duke, in 1986.

Not since the 14th century had a king of England been forced to abdicate, and the potters of England proved adept at converting many coronation wares into abdication pieces. Objects which bear both coronation and abdication inscriptions are particularly sought-after. By 1972, the furore surrounding the abdication had been largely forgotten, and the news of the Duke's death was greeted with relative indifference by the makers of commemoratives.

▲ Any memorial pieces for Edward's death are very rare. Coalport were the only major manufacturer to produce a memorial to the Duke. This plate, made in a limited edition of 1,000, has an attractive design with a central coat of arms printed in gilt and a purple border with three profile portrait silhouettes; the reverse is inscribed with a poignant epitaph by Churchill.

£150-200

▼ Like many of the commemoratives made for Edward's abdication, this inexpensive earthenware mug was originally produced as a coronation mug and was adapted for its new purpose. It has the additional information of the date of abdication hand painted on at a later date.

£50-70

► Although not particularly striking at first sight, this large Edward memorial mug is significant as it was the first ceramic piece also to feature the Duchess of Windsor. Made by Mercian China, these mugs cost just £6 when first sold.

£95

◄ This novelty musical jug is one of the more unusual pieces made for the King's intended coronation, and plays the song, "God Save The King". The jug was made by Fieldings pottery under the Crown Devon brand name, who continued to market the piece by adding the date of abdication; similar two-handled loving-cups with the same design were also produced. The distinctive pale honey glaze on the piece had been popularized by Clarice Cliff, who was another well-known pottery manufacturer at this time.

£100-150

► The black and white photographic portrait of the Duke of Windsor in his later days which decorates this plate is not very flattering. Nevertheless, the overall design is strong, and because items produced to commemorate the Duke's death are so scarce this example would still be sought-after among collectors.

£80-120

George VI
(1937-1952)

Prince Albert unexpectedly inherited the throne after the abdication of his brother in 1937. Shy and retiring and with a debilitating stutter, he was a sickly prince susceptible to gastric attacks and not well-suited to the demands placed on him by his surprise kingship. Following the royal tradition with second sons, he served in the Navy as a midshipman and after seeing active service in the First World War he left in 1920 and was made Duke of York by his father. He married Lady Elizabeth Bowes-Lyon in 1923 and they had two daughters, Elizabeth and Margaret. The young wife accepted her role as Queen nobly but could never forgive her brother-in-law for inflicting the role of King upon her husband. Three years after his coronation the Second World War broke out. The King and Queen touched the hearts of the nation when they stayed in London with their children rather than escaping abroad; it is said that when Buckingham Palace was bombed the Queen reported she was glad because she could now "look the East Enders in the Face".

Commemoratives made for the King's coronation are largely adaptations of those made for Edward VIII's coronation, as the event took place on the original date. The adaptation was not difficult for items without photographic prints, but was more challenging when the Queen's portrait had to be added. Generally, pieces for George VI's coronation are less interesting than those intended for

Edward VIII. George's mother and two daughters attended the ceremony and portraits of the family appear on a number of coronation wares. These tend to be taken from originals by the royal photographer, Marcus Adams, or the Court photographers Vandyk and Bassano. One of the most interesting items was a tyg made by the Bovey pottery commemorating 1936 as the "Year of the Three Kings" which bears a portrait of George V and Queen Mary, Edward VIII and George VI and Queen Elizabeth. The outbreak of the Second World War in 1939 restricted the potteries to producing utility wares for the home market and the very few colour-printed items that do appear were made for export. Most were made later, as at the time all the country's resources were needed for the war efforts. They usually feature the Prime Minister Winston Churchill and there are almost as many items bearing his portrait as there are the King's. After the war Utility China continued to be enforced, and was still in operation at the time of the King's death in 1952, making any pieces for his death extremely rare and desirable. The King's daughter, Elizabeth, married Prince Philip in 1947 and again there are only a handful of commemoratives to mark the event.

The most interesting and collectable are the limited editions produced by Minton (still in two-colour). Apart from a few pieces made by Wedgwood, Minton and Doulton for the King and Queen's visit to Canada in 1939, the only other commemoratives made were for the Festival of Britain in 1951. The Festival was the British attempt to restore optimism to the country by launching a new decade with a new approach to design and living. However, this was difficult to achieve when Utility China was still in force!

Left: *A fine gilded Paragon loving cup made for George VI's coronation, 1937.*

Above: *A Dame Laura Knight mug for George VI's coronation adapted from a design for Edward VIII's coronation, 1937.*

The Coronation
(1937)

The coronation of George VI took place on 12 May 1937, the day originally intended for the coronation of his brother, Edward VIII, who abdicated in December 1936. The abdication came as a complete shock to George and for a short time there was some uncertainty as to whether his younger brother, the Duke of Kent, should become King. George managed to overcome his inherent shyness, manifested by a severe speech impediment, and with the support of his Queen, Elizabeth Bowes-Lyon, he became a popular and astute King. His reign was a time of great political unrest in Europe, culminating in the Second World War.

Many potters adapted the designs they had produced for Edward VIII's prospective coronation to make them relevant to the new King – the two brothers were quite similar in appearance so the task was not always difficult. In general it was a very busy time for the potteries and the majority of them benefitted from the two coronations, unaware of the restrictions that were to be imposed on them after the outbreak of the Second World War three years later, when coloured wares could be produced only for export. The principal makers were Wedgwood, Coalport, Derby, Minton – and Royal Doulton who produced some of the best pieces.

▼ This Royal Crown Derby loving cup represents British pottery at its best. It is printed with fine-quality portraits of the King and Queen, and gilt has been used to decorate the elaborate foliate scroll handles and the interior bands of berries and laurel.

£250-300

▲ After the disintegration of Edward VIII's marriage, designers were keen to portray George VI with his wife and children to reaffirm the stability of the family. This mug is printed with a sepia print of the King and Queen with the two Princesses, after a photograph by Marcus Adams. The piece is marked Diamond China, the name of a lesser manufacturer based in Staffordshire. **£40-50**

► Among the smaller commemoratives for the coronation is this cigarette/match holder and ashtray made by Doulton at their Burslem factory which is decorated with their distinctive berry and laurel design.

£60-80

◀ Die-cast toys were made from metal formed under pressure in a mould by being passed between a steel die and a drop hammer. They were popularized in Britain by Meccano who introduced their Modelled Miniatures range in 1933 (which became Dinky toys a year later). These William Britain figures of the King and Queen in their coronation robes come in their original boxes which give details of their attire. Their excellent condition and the original boxes make them highly collectable. **£80-120 the pair**

▼ This set of silver plated teaspoons was produced for George VI's coronation. The finial of each teaspoon is cast as one of the monarchs of the century 1837-1937. They come in a fitted case printed in silk. The idea of figural decoration on spoons is derived from the Apostle spoons produced during the late middle ages, decorated with figures representing the Twelve Apostles. **£80-120**

► Wedgwood made an extensive and varied range of commemorative mugs, designed by a number of their key artists. The pottery is probably best-known for its range of jasperware, which it began to produce in c.1774, made of a stoneware body covered in a dense matt blue glaze. White relief-moulded decoration was then applied to the body. This jasperware mug has a profile of George VI on one side and of Queen Elizabeth on the other. It follows a design Wedgwood produced for a plaque. The King and Queen are informally dressed – the King is wearing mourning suit. Typically, this piece is impressed with the pottery's name, "Wedgwood made in England", and was made at their Etruria works.
£100-150

▼ A number of inexpensive loving cups were produced by unnamed makers for the coronation. This example is made in earthenware and bears a double moulded portrait of the King and Queen. The handles, elaborately moulded into the form of the year 1937, have been enamelled in simulated bronze.

£40-60

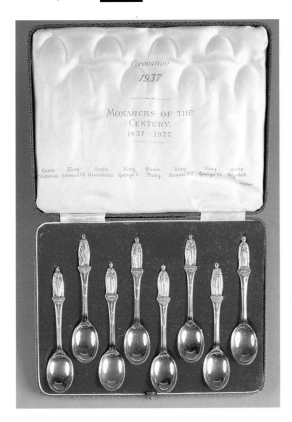

Royal Visits

When George VI and Elizabeth made an official trip to the United States and Canada in 1939 they were the first British monarchs to do so. The event was commemorated in many wares, including some commissioned by American retailers from Wedgwood and Minton. After the Second World War the King and Queen visited North Africa for 14 days but nothing exists to mark this visit, probably because of the restrictions on commemoratives at this time. In 1947 the couple went to South Africa with their two daughters. A visit was also planned to Australia and New Zealand in 1949 but this was never made because of the King's increasing ill health.

◄ This moulded jug with a straw glaze, made for the cancelled visit to Australia, is typically simple but the addition of coloured glazes suggest it was made for export.

£20-30

◄ ▲ Wedgwood were given an exclusive commission by W. H. Plummer and Co. Ltd. in New York to produce a limited edition of plates commemorating the royal couple's first visit to the United States in 1939. Unlike items in Wedgwood's dry-bodied jasper ware, these earthenware plates have been glazed in white and applied with pale blue glazed profile portraits of the King and Queen. The rims bear the American Eagle and the words "Friendship Makes Peace". The plate bearing the King's portrait is number 48 of 3,000 and that of the Queen number 141 of 3,000.

£250-350

▶ This simple mug with a semi-translucent honey glaze is typical of post-war commemoratives. It was made for the royal visit to South Africa in 1947.

£20-30

▼ Paragon made a number of wares to celebrate the royal visit to Canada. This cup and saucer has been colour printed with the distinctly Canadian motifs of maple leaves around the borders and the country's Royal Arms.

£40-50

▲ Several minor glassmakers in the Gateshead region produced beaded commemorative glassware. This plate was made for the cancelled Australian tour. **£30-40**

▼ This rare plate commemorating the royal visit to Canada and the United States depicts a double portrait of the King and Queen flanked by buildings from Ottawa and Washington.

£60-80

◀ The fact that this mug marking the King and Queen's visit to South Africa in 1947 is colour-printed indicates it was produced for export.

£20-30

World War II
(1939-45)

Very few Second World War commemoratives were produced (probably as few as 10% of those made for the First World War), as every resource was needed for the war effort. Many wares were patriotic, others were made on a lighter note – the Stoke-on-Trent firm of Fieldings produced a series of miniature chamber pots which had interiors printed with character portraits of Hitler, Mussolini and Göering, and exteriors bearing humorous slogans. As well as British heroes, a few items feature President Truman of the United States and Stalin of the Soviet Union.

THE BATTLE OF BRITAIN

The Battle of Britain is regarded by many as the turning point of the Second World War. It consisted of a series of air battles staged between Britain and Germany from August to October 1940. Initially, the Germans attempted to gain air control of British coastal areas, but gradually moved inland staging a number of night bombings on principal cities, beginning with the London blitz. The RAF made a gallant defence against the Germans who were gradually pushed back to the coasts, and the Battle of Britain became the first major British victory despite the German superiority in numbers. Britain's two saviours were the Spitfire and Hawker Hurricane aircraft which far excelled any fighter aircraft the Germans had and in the end the Germans lost 2,300 aircraft, the RAF only 900.

◀ *Spitfire* is one of a series of bone china figures made by Royal Worcester in 1941 and modelled by Eileen Soper. Depicting wartime children, they are highly collectable and rare today.
£2,000

▼ Second World War commemoratives often bear the now legendary words by Churchill that "Never was so much owed by so many to so few", which appears on this glazed earthenware wall plaque of a Spitfire. **£80-120**

▼ The Churchill quote also appears on this cup and saucer which forms part of a Patriotic Series of cups and saucers of a standard shape and size produced by Paragon. The fine-quality Royal Airforce insignia and two Spitfires are printed on a sky blue ground. Other examples in the series were made for the Royal Navy and these are printed with a compass motif; other ground colours include pale yellow or green.
£80-120

► Lord Montgomery is one of the most represented Second World War heroes to appear on commemoratives. This character jug of the leader in military uniform was probably made shortly after the war, in Staffordshire. Royal Doulton produced similar "Monty" character jugs many years later, and these continue to sell well for the pottery today.

£80-120

► Prime Ministers have always been popular subjects with the potters. Neville Chamberlain was Prime Minister when war was declared on Germany in 1939. This standard-quality character mug of Chamberlain was possibly made by the firm of Gibsons who is known to have made similar mugs at this time.

£60-90

GREAT LEADERS

• Winston Churchill (1874-1964) is renowned for his brilliant qualities of leadership in war. His rousing speeches and stubborn refusal to make peace with the Germans until Hitler was crushed sustained the British resistance. (See also pp.132-3.)

• Bernard Law Montgomery (1887-1976) commanded the British army in North Africa, Sicily and Italy between 1942 and 1944 and was commander in chief of the British Group of Armies and Allied Armies in Northern France in 1944. He was made Field Marshall and became a national hero after his achievements at the battle of El Alamein in Egypt in 1942 where he led the British army to drive the Germans back 2,000 miles (3,218 km) across Africa into Tunisia and took 30,000 prisoners, signalling the end for Germany.

• Neville Chamberlain (1869-1941) initially upheld Adolf Hitler as a great statesman who believed in peace, and in this belief he had signed the Munich Pact of appeasement in September 1938 which aimed to preserve peace in Europe. As Hitler became increasingly aggressive, Chamberlain realised he had been wrong about him. After the British debacle in Norway in 1940, he was forced to resign his leadership to Winston Churchill.

▲ This Spanish hand-painted figure of Churchill, very unusually shows him in airforce uniform which adds to the value. His pose here came to be his trademark – offering his right hand in the form of a "v" sign (for victory) and holding in his left hand his famous cigar. Examples also exist of Hitler and de Gaulle. £185

THE YALTA CONFERENCE

A conference was held in Yalta, Russia, from 4 to 11 February 1945 between the British Prime Minister Winston Churchill, the President of the United States Franklin D. Roosevelt, and the Soviet Premier Stalin. The leaders stipulated that the Germans surrender unconditionally and laid out terms for peace. Many of the details of the conference were not published until after the war, in 1947.

▲ These figures of Churchill, Roosevelt and Stalin were made by The Bovey Tracey Pottery Company, Devon. A white set was made for home consumption and an enamel-painted set of the three leaders was made for export. **£60-90 each**

▶ During the war toys were scarce as many toy makers had to switch their efforts to making more essential supplies. These two felt dolls of a male and female soldier have finely moulded heads and are dressed in khaki uniform. Because of their rarity they are highly collectable.

£100-150

▲ This moulded mug of General Eisenhower was probably produced in the United States. **£60-90**

▲ This RAF Benevolent Fund bell was made with metal reclaimed from German aircraft shot down over Britain. **£30-50**

▲ ▼ A number of commemoratives were produced both in Britain and the United States portraying American wartime leaders. These two plates form part of the Allied Nations Commemorative Series which was produced in the United States. Each one follows the same pattern, with sepia prints of the leaders surrounded by brightly coloured borders of flags. These two portraits are of General Marshall and Franklin Roosevelt; another example exists with the portrait of General Eisenhower.

£150-200

◄ British makers produced a number of wares for the American market. This Wedgwood jasperware plate bears a profile portrait of President Roosevelt, and was possibly made during the war.

£70-90

▼ This rare pottery cup and saucer was made on 3 September 1939 to mark the outbreak of the war. Although by an unknown maker, it is still worth between £50 and £70.

Elizabeth's Wedding (1947)

When George VI's daughter, Princess Elizabeth, married Lieutenant Philip Mountbatten (Prince Philip of Greece) on 20 November 1947 the nation was finally given something to celebrate after the gloom that followed the aftermath of the Second World War. These were austere years and the pottery industry had been severely restricted. Until 1950 rationing was still imposed on the British public and in deference to this the Royal Family had to stage a less ostentatious wedding than usual. Consequently, very few commemoratives were made for the wedding and many of those that were produced are quite drab, as all multi-coloured wares had to be exported to boost the British economy.

◄ This impressive bone china Minton vase was made in a limited edition of 500 and is one of the most collectable items produced for the royal wedding. The cylindrical form is redolent of the best Art Deco designs of the 1930s. The body is divided into panels printed in gilt with the initials "EP". The central panel bears the royal coat of arms and is flanked on either side by rose, thistle and shamrock sprays. Examples exist without the gilding. The inscription to the couple on the base follows Minton's practice of signing all its prestige wears in gilt. **£600-900**

◄ Only two pottery manufacturers are thought to have made commemoratives for the wedding of Elizabeth and Prince Philip (Minton, *above*, and the Ewenny Pottery in South Wales). However, the event was recorded in a variety of other media. This cake stand is typical of the less expensive pieces produced. The transfer is crooked, the glass base is cheap and the handle has been plated in chrome.

£30-50

The Festival of Britain
(1951)

The last major event of George VI's reign was the Festival of Britain, planned to take place a hundred years after the Great Exhibition of 1851 which had been held in Hyde Park. This time an old bomb site on the south Bank was chosen for the exhibition (including the new Royal Festival Hall) as the intention was to display the products of the new Britain that had emerged out of the debris of the Second World War. King George opened the Festival on 2 May from the steps of St Paul's Cathedral. There are few exhibition commemoratives available today, but the range was varied – from inexpensive souvenirs such as badges, to liqueur sets, tablewares and the crown (five shilling piece) specially made for the event.

▲ This matchbox printed with a photograph of Shakespeare's birthplace reflects the growing interest in tourism in Britain. Like other Festival items, it bears the symbol of a compass.
£10-15

▲ This marmalade pot could be just another 1930's piece if not for the addition of the Festival of Britain label.
£15-25

► A number of jade green glazed ceramics commemorate the Festival. The nice simple design of this dish in the form of a half penny piece gives it a relatively high value.
£35-45

▲ The compass symbol of the Festival appears on a number of commemoratives, including this souvenir drinking glass which was probably part of a liqueur set. It is fairly unremarkable and therefore inexpensive.
£10-15

Sir Winston Churchill
(1874-1965)

Winston Churchill was born in 1874, the son of Lord Randolph Churchill and an American, Jennie Jerome. A great statesman, leader and recognized author (he was awarded the Nobel Prize for Literature in 1953), he is particularly famous for his contribution to Britain's success in the Second World War (see pp. 126-8). He was Prime Minister between 1940 and 1945 and 1951 and 1955, and First Lord of the Admiralty from 1911 to 1915 and 1939 to 1940. He cemented very close ties with the United States and had a particularly good relationship with President Roosevelt, with whom he appears on a number of commemoratives. He was also instrumental in sealing the alliance between Britain, America and Russia in 1941. Most commemoratives were made immediately after the war when Churchill was at the height of his fame (despite losing the first post-war election to Clement Atlee and the Labour party); other items were made when he became Prime Minister for the second time, and on his death in 1965, when he became the first person outside of the monarchy to appear on a coin. Today Churchill provides one of the most popular collecting areas and even his cigars, letters and signatures are sought after. The rarest items are "wanted" posters from his period of capture during the Boer War in 1899.

▼ Black basalt was a popular material for mourning wares. Made from a mixture of fine Dorset clay and manganese which was fired twice and left unglazed, it was very versatile and adapted easily to both moulded and applied decoration. Josiah Wedgwood was the first person to produce black basalts successfully, in the 1770s, and such wares, often known as "Egyptian Black", soon became the staple of a number of lesser-known factories in Staffordshire. This circular plate with a moulded profile portrait of Churchill and gilt lettering is one of the finer quality pieces made to commemorate the leader's life.

£60-90

▼ The figure of Churchill was not confined to ceramics: his portrait appeared on a number of other items including matchbox covers (made in a series which also included President Roosevelt); and dolls were made in his likeness. This one was probably made by Peggy Nisbet of Somerset, England, whose range includes a limited edition of 1,000 Prince Charles and Diana wedding dolls. This doll is dressed in Churchill's Order of the Knight of the Garter robes and like many post-war dolls, has a material body and celluloid head.

£80-120

▼ Churchill's rousing speeches are frequently quoted and are printed on many ceramics. This Wedgwood tankard bears the inscription "Give us the tools and we'll finish the job" together with a lengthy Churchill quote on the base. It was probably made at the pottery's Barleston factory which opened during the early years of the Second World War. **£50**

▲ This cup was made by the firm of Burleigh. It is highly collectable as the base shows Chruchill and Roosevelt holding hands, marking Churchill's importance in securing Anglo-American relations. **£200-300**

► Although the majority of character jugs were made by the minor potteries, this example of Churchill was produced by Clarice Cliff for Wilkinson Ltd. In design and style it has more in common with a number of character mugs of political and military personalities from the First World War produced for Wilkinson by Carruthers Gould, than with Cliff's usual production. The leader is dressed as the Warden of the Cinque Ports and is seated on a bulldog, draped with a Union Jack (a pun, as Churchill was well-known for his bulldog personality and appearance).

£400-500

Elizabeth II
(1952 - present)

Elizabeth's reign has been a period of great change. In the Commonwealth it has seen the final disbanding of the British colonies overseas and the subsequent independence of its members, such as Tanzania, Jamaica, the African States, Ghana, the Caribbean and Canada. Great technological and scientific advances have been made: man landed on the moon; nuclear energy was discovered after the splitting of the atom; the first successful heart transplant operation was carried out; and the first test tube baby was born. The threat of nuclear war has been a near reality on several occasions, perhaps most notably during the Suez Canal crisis in 1956, and the Cuban Missile Crisis in 1963 when President Kennedy of the United States put the world on nuclear alert. More recent troubles include the

Falklands War and terrorism in Northern Ireland. It has also been a time of optimism; the Cold War with Russia has thawed and the Berlin Wall is no longer a divide between East and West Germany. In recent years the question of the need for a monarchy has been raised, particularly following the increasing matrimonial problems of the Queen's children. These have dispelled some of the myths surrounding the family and, unfortunately, lost them some respect. Now, although people are still fascinated by the glamour associated with the royal family, they are equally interested in their increasingly public scandals.

Elizabeth II was the first monarch to have her coronation watched on television by thousands of subjects both in Britain and throughout the Commonwealth. Commemoratives tend to be relatively unadventurous despite the fact that they have been made in vast quantities. The Queen's image appears on anything from chocolate boxes, tins, cards and printed souvenirs to silver-plated spoons, pottery, and British coinage, where she is in the uniform she wears when attending the trooping the colours. A massive amount of paraphernalia was produced for her coronation. In ceramics, styles echo those which have dominated since the coronation of George V;

Wedgwood's wares are some of the most collectable. After the coronation, the next significant family event – the marriage of her sister Margaret to Anthony Armstrong Jones in 1960 – is commemorated by an elegant cup and saucer by Paragon. Prince Charles's investiture at Caernarvon, Wales in 1969 was the next real celebration – pageants were held throughout the country and many souvenirs produced. The marriage of Princess Anne to Mark Phillips a few years later was marked by the usual everyday commemoratives, as were the successive events of the Queen's Jubilee in 1977 and the marriages of her children and the births of her grandchildren. The far greater number of items for Elizabeth than for earlier monarchs reflects the length of her reign and the improving economy – people today tend to have more income to spend on souvenirs than previously. Attempts have been made to control standards in production, but there is still much of debatable quality around. In general, items for the insignificant small events are the most desirable. As with many modern collectables they are worth buying today as they give continuity to a collection and value will increase in time. Because they are inexpensive, they can be bought by people with even the most modest incomes.

Left: A Wedgwood mug designed by Richard Guyatt for the silver wedding anniversary of the Queen and Duke of Edinburgh, 1972.

Above : A blue jasperware Wedgwood teapot made for the Queen's coronation, 1953.

The Coronation
(1953)

The coronation of Elizabeth II was held at London's Westminister Abbey on 2 June 1953. It was the first coronation to be televised (the Queen overruled her advsors' wishes to the contrary) and this added 20 million viewers to the 30,000 spectators lining the Mall. It was also the first time a monarch was crowned without a partner – Philip had agreed not to take an active role in the constitution. Elizabeth was attended by her small children, Anne and Charles, Queen Mary and Queen Elizabeth the Queen's mother. Winston Churchill also attended. The Queen travelled to the Abbey in the tradtional Gold State Coach, which weighs four tons and was drawn by eight horses. It was built in 1762 for King George III and had been used for every coronation since William IV's in 1831. Many of the chairs and stools used at the ceremony have since surfaced at auction.

▲ A number of American firms produced wares to commemorate the Queen's coronation. The colourful half portrait of the Queen on this square canted plate was painted by Allen Huabes.

£25-30

▲ This limited edition coronation glass goblet was made by Whitefriars in Wealdstone, Middlesex and harks back to the shapes the firm produced back in the 18th century. The bowl is engraved with a cypher and the date under a crown. The stem has been colourfully enamelled with a white spiral entwined with red and blue curves.

£80-100

▶ This Tuscan ware bone china plate by a Staffordshire maker has an attractive photographic portrait of the Queen and is one of the better pieces made to mark the coronation.

£50-70

▲ This Queen Ellizabeth II coronation mug has been adapted from a design by Eric Ravilious. It was originally conceived for the coronation of Edward VIII, then redesigned for George VI, and used again here – posthumously, as Ravilious died whilst working as a war artist during the Second World War.

£200-300

► The Staffordshire firm of Crown Ducal made this fine plate which is printed with a particularly good photographic image of the Queen.

£350-450

▼ This St Ives mug is only one of a few studio pottery pieces made for the coronation. **£80-120**

▼ Plaster figures were produced as less expensive alternatives to the Staffordshire pottery figures of the 1930s. The colours are unstable and the piece is liable to crack under excessive heat.

£30-50

▼ This Doulton mug was made in three shapes: the straight-sided mug was most common and examples with a fluted base most rare; others were in the form of a beaker. The photograph is by the artist, Dorothy Wilding. A similar version exists with a portrait of Elizabeth as princess. **£40-60 each**

▼ Since the coronation of George VI any seating provided for peers of the realm and other notables invited to the coronation has been sold afterwards. Stools, such as this one, are less desirable than chairs. Typically, this piece is upholstered in blue/grey velvet and has a cypher in one corner. On the underside is a brand mark, confirming its use at the coronation.

£80-120

▲ ▲ Tins for tea, biscuits, chocolates and various other groceries were produced in abundance to celebrate the Queen's coronation. Most bear a single photographic portrait of Elizabeth, but others include Prince Philip and their children. Condition is important to value. Although the cream-coloured tin bears a better portrait than the blue one, the fact that it is rather rusty will lower the price. The blue tin bears an inscription saying it contains one pound of chocolates made by J. Lyons and Co. Ltd of Cadby Hall, London W14. The portrait is by Dorothy Wilding.

£30-40 each

▼ Among the wide variety of printed ephemera made for the coronation is this *Debrett's Dictionary of the Coronation* which would have provided the definitive word on protocol at the ceremony. Other items include souvenir programmes and prayer books.

£30-50

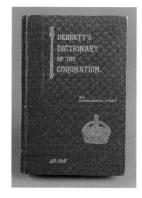

The Moon Landing
(1969)

When American astronauts Neil Armstrong, Edwin Aldrin Jnr and Michael Collins set foot on the moon at 3.56am BST on 21 July 1969 they signalled the greatest advance in science in the 20th century, proving man's determination to master the universe. The event was transmitted live by satellite to millions of viewers around the world and was commemorated in a variety of media. The mainstream ceramic wares included jasperware plates by Wedgwood and the blue and white wares of Royal Copenhagen, as well as a plethora of items by lesser known manufacturers, the majority in the United States.

► One of the more unusual items made to commemorate man's landing on the moon is this Aynsley globe. Decorated in gilt with the stars and stripes of the United States, it celebrates the event as the greatest achievement of the age.

£80-100

▼ The Apollo Soyuz Space Mission in 1975 involved the linkup in space of the American and Russian spacecrafts. Up until this time American and Russian space programmes had been developed independently, which meant the two schemes were not compatible. For the Soyuz Mission both space ships were modified so that the linkup could take place. This special commemorative pack includes a first day cover stamp produced for the event and a limited edition proof coin in Sterling silver.

£50-70

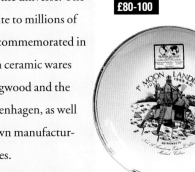

▲ Ceramic plates were made in quantity for the landing. The decoration on this one includes a copy of the plaque that was left on the moon bearing the names of the astronauts and of President Nixon.

£30-40

► Engraved glass lent itself particularly well to commemorating the landing on the moon. This fine Caithness bowl is number 3 in a limited edition of 12.

£250-350

The 1969 Investiture

The investiture of Prince Charles as the 21st Prince of Wales took place at Caernarvon Castle in Wales on 1 July 1969. It was the first investiture to be televised in colour and provided a great spectacle. The castle was adorned with pennants and banners and a mixture of modern and traditional designs by Lord Snowdon. The event was swamped with commemoratives as this was the first event worth celebrating since the Queen's coronation. The best items were those produced by the premier pottery manufacturers, Wedgwood, Royal Crown Derby and Doulton. As with the coronation, chairs used as the event were sold as collector's items – a red-lacquered example with Prince of Wales feathers in gold on the back was sold for around £100 in the 1980s.

▼ ▲ Mugs for the investiture vary greatly in quality and value. The bone china mug above is colourful and is ornately decorated with good gilding. On one side is an elaborate coat of arms and on the other a list of the past Princes of Wales. Because it is of fine quality and was made by the reputable firm of Aynsley it is worth £70-90.

The mug below bears the common design of a rather unflattering photograph of the Prince and is worth only £30.

▶ The red dragon depicted in this high quality limited edition Royal Crown Derby figure is the emblem of Wales. The fine modelling and lavish gilt decoration make this figure an even more desirable piece.

£500-600

▼ After Wedgwood's discovery and development of jasper, the firm produced a succession of jasper portrait medallions and plaques. Among the historical and political personalities depicted were members of the royal family from the reign of George III onwards. These are highly collectable today, both in Britain and the United States.

£100-150

▲ The Welsh dragon and the Prince of Wales feathers feature on a vast range of wares made for the 1969 investiture but this mug, designed by Richard Guyatt, is of particularly high quality. One of the most innovative designers of the 1960s and '70s, Guyatt produced a number of designs in a similar style to mark various royal events. This pint-sized mug is lettered in Welsh. Other examples were made by Guyatt for the Silver Wedding Anniversary of the Queen and Prince Philip in 1972 and for the marriage of Princess Anne and Captain Mark Phillips (see

£80-120

▶ This Wedgwood money box in the colours of the Welsh flag was one of the most popular items made for the investiture. Although the form is complex, the decoration is fairly restrained.

£35-45

▲ This Capo-Di-Monte figure of Prince Charles is one of the best items produced outside of Britain to commemorate his investiture, and at 14 in (38cm) high is also one of the largest figures of Charles ever made. It has been intricately modelled and bears a good likeness to the Prince – who is wearing the crown designed for him by Lord Snowdon.

£300-400

Family Life

The country's loyalty to Queen Elizabeth has always been strong and the lives of her family have been followed with keen interest. However, apart from the wedding and coronation wares, there are relatively few commemoratives around. The births of royal children are popular, particularly those of Elizabeth's younger sons, Andrew and Edward, who were born after her coronation. Birthdays are also popular, especially those of the Queen Mother (see pp. 162-3), and the deaths of members of the royal family are also duly recorded.

▲ Sepia prints, popular during the Victorian age, underwent a revival during the reign of Queen Elizabeth. This Caverswall mug was made for Prince Andrew's 21st birthday. His naval background is reflected in the decorative border.

£50-60

▼ This Paragon plate bears an attractive sepia photographic portrait of Prince Charles as a young boy taken by the court photographer, Marcus Adams, whose photographs have gained a rapid increase in popularity with collectors in recent years. Sepia photographs can be found on commemoratives beginning with the reign of George IV and covering members of the royal family right up to the present day. This example was produced at the time of the coronation.

£60-90

▲ These glass plates bear portraits of Charles and Anne, and were probably made at the time of the Queen's coronation in 1957. Similar plates exist for the wedding of Elizabeth and Philip. The photographs were possibly taken by the royal portraitist, Dorothy Wilding. **£60-80 a pair**

▼ The lives of more distant members of the royal family are also commemorated. This mug for the death of the Duchess of Windsor who died at her home in Paris in 1986 is very rare and this will add to its value.

£40-60

► When Queen Victoria's great grandson, the First Earl Mountbatten of Burma, was killed by an IRA bomb in 1979, the country was outraged. He was a well-respected figure and his death spawned a number of commemoratives. This plate provides a documentary of Mountbatten's life, including his service in the navy and his appointment as Viceroy of India in 1947.

£80-120

▼ The death in 1981 of Queen Victoria's last surviving granddaughter, Princess Alice, was sadly mourned. This very rare porcelain mug made by John May to commemorate the Princess's death is a typical funeral piece – decorated in purple with black lettering, and with a neo-Baroque cartouche and Gothic writing.

£40-60

▲ Two designs of mug were made for the death of Mountbatten. This example, commissioned by John May, is particularly poignant, as the insription describes Mountbatten as having been "murdered". The other mug, by Panorama, bears a black and white portrait of the Earl and a description of his murder.

£25-45

▼ Wedgwood's black basalt was often used for funeral wares. This portrait medallion of Mountbatten was made for his death in a limited edition of 500 and is highly collectable today.

£100-150

▲ This mug was made by A & C Dorincort in a limited edition of 150 to mark the delegation of Princess Anne as the Princess Royal on 13 June 1987 (and was later adapted for her 40th birthday). On the reverse is a black and white portrait of the Princess. It is tastefully lettered in gilt, in the manner of an invitation card.

£40-50

The Marriage of Princess Anne & Captain Mark Phillips
(1973)

Princess Anne was the first of Elizabeth's children to marry. The wedding took place on 14 November 1973 at Westminster Abbey, and compared with the marriage of the future King and Queen, Prince Charles and Lady Diana Spencer, it was a fairly subdued affair. It was heralded as "the perfect marriage" and many commemoratives made for the event set the happy couple against an idealistic romantic setting. Princess Anne was not the most popular member of the royal family and the public did not fall in love with Mark Phillips as they did with Diana and consequently far fewer commemoratives were produced. As with most other royal occasions, pottery wares are the most abundant, produced in varying degrees of quality, and mainly as cabinet pieces rather than as useful wares. Those produced by Wedgwood are especially sought after in the United States. Particularly interesting to collectors are commemoratives with an obviously 1970's look and style.

► This Aynsley plate is printed with the same photographic portrait as appears on the cup and bell on the opposite page, but it is made more interesting by the addition of the blue gilded border and horseshoe and bell wedding motifs encircling Anne and Mark's initials.

£35

▼ A number of lesser-known factories produced commemoratives for the wedding. This mug was commissioned by the firm of Wilson's in Paignton, Devon, as one of a pair with another bearing a black and white print of Mark Phillips. The Union Jack flag on this example has been used on commemorative wares since the reign of Queen Victoria.

£15-25

▲ This fine Wedgwood tankard with a balanced shape and busy composition, was designed by Richard Guyatt as a cabinet piece.

£40-50

► This flimsy silver-coloured metal tray has been lithoprinted with an unattractive portrait of **Princess Anne** and **Captain Mark Phillips**. The design is of dubious quality and the tray is a good example of the vast range of inexpensive commemoratives that were produced for the couple's marriage.

£20-25

▼▲ Aynsley made a standard range of bone china for the wedding, all bearing an identical printed photographic portrait of the couple. These pieces had general populist appeal and could be bought relatively inexpensively by the patriotic public. This table bell is purely decorative and would have been bought to display in a cabinet.

bell £40, beaker £20-30

▼ This mug was produced for the mass market and is very much a 1970s' design (the flowers in the Princess's hair are redolent of the "flower power" years). The novelty composition places **Anne** and **Mark** within a heart-shaped cartouche surrounded by images of horses and Westminster Abbey, where the couple were married. The thick body and bright rim suggest the mug was intended for use, not display.

£20-30

▲ This plate was made in a limited edition by the firm of **Crown Staffordshire**. It is highly unusual in not incorporating a portrait of the couple into the decoration and is not one of the firm's best designs. This is reflected in the relatively low price compared to other pieces made by them.

£20-30

Political Strife

There was great political unrest in Britain after the Second World War, made worse by a rapidly changing economy. Britain's status as a superpower was diminishing – in the 1950s and '60s many Commonwealth States were granted their own autonomy – and the country's position was undermined by the Suez Crisis in 1956. Britain passed between successive Labour and Conservative governments as the public lost faith in its leaders. Harold Wilson, elected Labour Prime Minister in 1964, tried to strengthen Britain's position in Europe; he also imposed strict controls on wages and prices and devalued the pound to try and revive the ailing economy. Despite his success, Wilson suffered a surprising defeat when he called an election in 1970, and Edward Heath and the Conservatives came to power. Heath secured Britain's entry into the Common Market in 1973 (see p. 148) and also tried to limit immigration into the country from the Commonwealth. Mounting inflation forced him to reinstate Wilson's wage controls and this led to the miners' strike between November 1973 and February 1974. Heath resigned and Wilson became Prime Minister again in 1974. Faced with further crises, particularly in Northern Ireland, he too resigned, in 1976, and was replaced by James Callaghan. It was not until Margaret Thatcher came to power in 1979 that any hope was restored to the country's low morale.

▼ John F. Kennedy was President of the United States between 1961 and 1963. He secured good East West relations, and his forward-thinking policies made him popular at home and abroad, particularly with the young. His one fall from popularity was his involvement in the Vietnam War. This plate was made for his assassination in 1963.

£50-70

▲ This "Gurgling Jug" is a caricature of Conservative leader, Edward Heath. He is clothed in naval outfit, possibly referring to his victory in the Admiral's Cup in his ship, the *Morning Cloud*.

£50-70

◀ This plate, printed with a black and white photograph of Harold Wilson, Labour Prime Minister between 1964 and 1970, and 1974 and 1976, was made in a limited edition by the Panorama Studios Limited.

£40-60

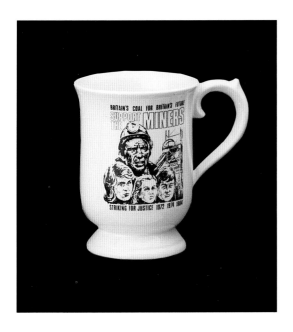

◄ **Political confrontations are always popular subjects on ceramics. This mug was made to commemorate the miners' strike in 1973/4 during Edward Heath's term in government, when the country was forced to work a three day week. Like many contemporary political commemoratives, the price of this piece is bound to rise.**

£40-50

▲ **When Mikhail Gorbachov succeeded Konstantin Chernenko as General Secretary of the Communist Party in the Soviet Union in 1985 it signalled the end of "old guard" Russian leadership and the Cold War. Gorbachov's policies of** *glasnost* **(openness) and** *perestroika* **(restructuring) opened the way for closer relations with the United Kingdom and the United States. This beautifully modelled character jug of the Russian President made to celebrate the end of the Cold War is one of a series by Kevin Frances Ceramics in Staffordshire (see p.158).**

£100-150

▼ **This mug was commissioned by the newspaper, the** *Observer.* **It bears a portrait of the Queen together with the portraits of the seven Prime Ministers of her government from the beginning of her reign up until her jubilee, from Winston Churchill, to James Callaghan, Labour Prime Minister 1976-1979.**

£30-50

▼ **Treatment of political figures by the media has become far less kind with more recent governments, particularly after the emergence of Fluck and Law's** *Spitting Image* **caricatures developed in the 1980s for their television programme. Popular subjects for their cruel treatment include Roy Hattersley, below right, who was elected Deputy Leader of the Labour Government under Neil Kinnock in 1983, and the 1990 Conservative Prime Minister, John Major, below left. Others are the former Prime Minister, Margaret Thatcher. All these items are relatively inexpensive at the moment, but they will increase in value because they will appeal to the public's love of nostalgia.**

£20-30 each

The 1970s: A New Europe, A New Coinage

In the 1970s Britain made two significant decisions which brought the country in line with the rest of Europe. Following centuries of imperial coinage, on 15 February 1971 the British government voted to replace the old pounds, shillings and pence with a decimal system. Not all the old coins were defunct, as some were used to represent a new value – the old two shilling piece became the new ten pence piece.

A year later, on 9 January 1972, Britain, together with Ireland, Denmark and Norway, voted to join the Common Market. This was not a party decision, and Labour, Conservative and Liberal members all voted in its favour. Previous applications under both previous Labour and Conservative governments had been met with resistance from De Gaulle and the French government.

A number of wares were made to commemorate Britain's joining of the Common Market. This fine quality plate was commissioned for Mulberry Hall in York as a purely decorative item. Its rarity makes it expensive.

£80-120

▲ To mark the changing over of currency in the United Kingdom, souvenir sets of both the old and new coinage were issued by the Royal Mint. These coins were hermetically sealed in perspex and are in mint condition. Although quite interesting, they were issued in such vast numbers that they are of little collectable value today.

£10-15 a set

COMMEMORATED EVENTS

January 1972: "Bloody Sunday" in Londonderry when 13 civilians were killed in the continuing unrest in Northern Ireland.

September 1972: The Olympic Games were held in Munich. Arab guerrillas took Israeli atheletes hostage, killing them in a gun battle with police at the German airport of Fürstenfeldbruk.

February 1973: The Common Agricultural Policy (CAP) was brought into operation, giving a common policy to EEC farmers.

1974: A series of pub bombings on mainland Britain by the IRA killed and injured many civilians.

The Silver Jubilee
(1977)

The country hadn't had a jubilee to celebrate since the reign of George V and consequently in 1977 the market was deluged with commemoratives, especially as the royal family was then enjoying unprecedented popularity. The day was declared a national holiday and a service of thanksgiving was given. A committee was set up to decide whether objects were suitable and designs for all commemoratives were subjected to quality control. However, no stamp was issued to show whether an item had been approved. As usual, ceramics were the principal items produced, and all the premier manufactures were making wall plaques and mugs to commemorate the event. Other items included match boxes, playing cards, bookmarks, biscuit tins and chocolate boxes.

▲ A whole range of games were produced for the Jubilee. Waddingtons made a series of jigsaw puzzles to commemorate the event. The game on the left is particularly interesting as it depicts postage stamps from all around the world bearing the Queen's portrait and those of other members of the royal family. The one on the right is in mint condition and still in its cellophane packaging.

£10-15 each

◄ This well-designed bone china plate by Wedgwood follows the traditional style of commemorative wares. Colourfully-printed and lavishly decorated in gilt, it is one of the more collectable items.

£100-150

► This limited edition Mulberry Hall mug is one of a number of commemoratives sold by mail order. It has a sumptuous design and fine gilding around the lettering. **£60-80**

▲ Crown Staffordshire made this wall plate decorated with a fine photographic portrait of the Queen. The border of stylized laurel leaves is edged with a classical anthemion rim and is lavishly gilded. Because it was made in a limited edition it is worth between £60 and £90.

▼ Very few items were actually made to celebrate the 25 years from the Queen's coronation in 1953 – most take the date from her accession to the throne in 1952. This Coalport mug is therefore highly collectable. The interesting colour print bears the dates 1953-1978.

£20-30

▲ The modern print on this mug was very popular and, because it was produced in large numbers it can still be found in quantities today at affordable prices. It is still collectable because it is evocative of the 1970s style.

£10-15

▲ Colour photographic portraits of the Queen and Prince Philip have been printed on a number of packs of playing cards in recent years. Because this double pack commemorating the Silver Jubilee is in good condition the value will be considerably higher than if the set were damaged.

£10-15

▲ Toys provide another exciting and varied area for collectors of royal commemoratives. This model of the Queen in the State coach was made by the British firm of Mettoy Co. Ltd who made a number of die-cast Corgi toys from the 1960s onwards. Examples such as this, which is still in its original box, command a premium. The box is labelled in German and French as well as English, which reflects one of the changes brought about by Britain joining the Common Market (see p. 148) – Britain now produced wares to be sold in the member countries as well as at home.

£20-30

◀ This woven silk book-mark illustrates the variety and range of wares that were produced for the Queen's Silver Jubilee. This example follows the same traditional form as bookmarks produced in the reign of Queen Victoria by Thomas Stevens. It has been woven with part of an ode by the poet laureate, John Masefield and is still in good condition.

▲ This mug was made by Wedgwood for the Queen's visit to Germany to review the British troops at Fennelager on 7 July 1977.

£15-20

£20-30

▲ Die-cast models of the State coach have been popular since the time of the intended coronation of Edward VIII, when such toys were rapidly adapted for George VI by adding the figure of his wife. These cannot be confused with those for Elizabeth II's coronation as now the Queen, not the King, is wearing a crown. This model, in a box stamped with the official jubilee crown motif, is less interesting as there are no figures with it.

£20-30

▲ This plate was produced by Coalport, a premier English company which is now re-sited in Stoke on Trent. However, unlike many of their commemoratives, this example, printed with pictures of the royal residences, is not one of their most collectable. Commemoratives that feature portraits of the royal family tend to fetch higher prices than examples such as this which has an alternative design.

£60-80

The Marriage Of Prince Charles And Lady Diana Spencer
1981

When Prince Charles announced his engagement to Diana Spencer he ended years of speculation both at home and abroad. His choice of an "English rose" found good favour with the British public. It was a fairytale wedding, with the Princess walking down the aisle at St Paul's wearing a beautiful romantic dress designed by David and Elizabeth Emmanuel. The day was seen as an opportunity for the British to display their wealth, as the event was seen by millions throughout the world. It was also a chance to capitalize on all the tourists in London at the time and a host of commemorative objects were produced, ranging from pop-up books to biscuit tins. The usual vast array of ceramics appeared, from satirical pieces to the sophisticated fine bone china which constitutes some of the more expensive items on the market. Collectors have proved keen to hang on to their Charles and Di mementos, perhaps in the hope of their improving in price, but there is still a lot available, as so much was made. Prices are moderate so even children can afford to start a collection. In general, Charles and Di memorabilia has risen gradually in value and will continue to do so in the future, particularly as now the happy marriage has sadly come to an end.

▲ One of the finest Charles and Di items is this cobalt blue Royal Crown Derby loving cup made to a traditional Georgian design. Undoubtedly, the price is enhanced by the high quality of the decoration and gilding which proudly displays the Prince of Wales feathers and the arms of the Spencer family.

£300-500

▲ Printed ephemera provides an ideal collecting area for the more restricted pocket. This Holy Bible is an inexpensive memento of the royal marriage.   **£10-15**

▲ This pop-up book may have novelty value but has only a nominal monetary value. The fairytale romance of the Prince and Princess is told in movable parts, although the clumsy limitations of pop-up books have unfortunately turned Prince Phillip's hand wave into a salute reminiscent of a past dictator! **£20-30**

▼ This caricature of Diana shows her in the riding gear she wore on a visit to Canada. It was modelled by Douglas Tootle and although not a very good likeness of the Princess, it is a fun item that would be treasured by fans of Diana. Its value is increased as it was made in limited numbers.

£100-150

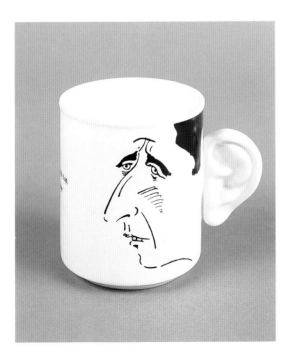

◀ Caricaturists like Fluck and Law have spared no one in their satirical treatment, least of all the royal family. This item designed by Mark Boxer ("Marc") makes a mug out of Prince Charles, with its ear handle and caricature-like cartoon that shows scant respect for the future king.

£15-25

▼ Tankards are always popular with collectors and this example is particularly desirable as it is made in pewter. The shape is traditional and the design simple, bearing a royal crest and an inscription of the date of the couple's marriage.

£20-30

► Biscuit tins produced to commemorate royal events are always worth more if they still have their original contents, so collectors will have to restrain themselves! The shield-shaped colour photograph of Diana and Charles on this example, which is held in place by two happy-looking lions, was taken on the actual day of the royal couple's engagement and has been reproduced on a number of other items made for the royal wedding.

£10-20

◄ Sepia photography with its nostalgic sentiment enjoyed a comeback at the time of the royal wedding. The flattering results can be seen in the central portraits of Charles and Diana on this limited edition Caverswall bone china plate, made in a quantity of only 2,500. Of added interest are views of Caernarvon Castle and the Spencer residence of Althorp.

£40-60

▼ This attractive and well-decorated loving cup is typical of Paragon royal commemoratives. The gilded lion handles are not unique to this piece, but appear on a range of their other wares. The tasteful portrait of the Prince and Princess shows them in relaxed and informal mood.

£200-300

▼ A huge amount of royal wedding mass produced goods flooded the market, so anything rare and individual will always be very desirable. This pair of silhouettes by Elizabeth Baverstock is probably unique and therefore commands a good price. The innovative use of a lace and fabric collage enhances its appeal, as does Princess Diana's characteristic downward gaze, complete with curling eyelashes.

£100-200

▼ In contrast to the simple design on the plate on the previous page, the decoration on this example is too fussy – the elaborate basket-weave reserves surrounding the couple's portraits only confuse the design.

£10-15

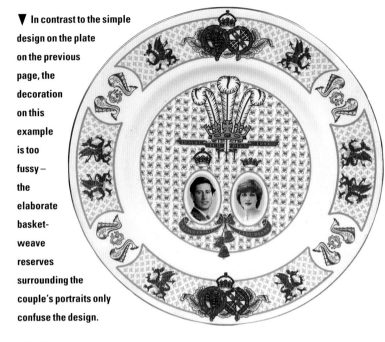

▼ Doulton have produced limited edition figures of members of the royal family throughout the 20th century. These bone china figures of Lady Diana and Prince Charles were made in limited numbers of 1,500 each and each one bears a registration number. They are of exceptionally high quality with very fine and detailed decoration and will increase in value over the years.   **£200-300 each**

▲ A number of breweries over the century have produced special brews to commemorate royal events. Among those featured here are a Royal Wedding Strong Lager and a Royal Celebration Ale; others were made for the Silver Jubilee. Although these are fun items, they are of nominal value today.

£10-15 each

Royal Visits

Members of the British Empire have gradually been given their independence since the Statute of Westminster was passed in Parliament in 1931. This paved the way for the Commonwealth of Nations whereby each dominion in the British Empire was granted autonomy, but bound to Britain through allegiance to the throne. As a result, the Queen, or sometimes an appointed agent, was frequently called to attend the independence celebrations of each newly emergent nation. As head of the Commonwealth the Queen has to play an active role in its smooth-running, as well as providing a centre of continuity for its members. There is hardly a country she has not visited, and to facilitate her visits the Queen has her own personal jet plane, and the *Royal Yacht Britannia,* aboard which she frequently entertains members of a host nation.

▲ **The Queen's children, Charles and Anne, are still very young on the sepia photograph on this mug made for a visit by the Queen to Jamaica. This suggests it was made in the early '50s, but this does not necessarily mean the visit dates to that time, as an old print could have been used.**

£25

▼ **The text on this simple mug details the Queen's visit to Canada in 1982 during which the Proclamation of Canada Act was signed. The sparse and uninspiring design of a red maple leaf on a white background makes the mug relatively inexpensive compared to items made by potteries like Mintons.**

£15

◀ **The Queen went to Australia and New Zealand as part of her Silver Jubilee tour in 1977. This plate commemorating the visit is decorated with typical New Zealand motifs of a kiwi bird, duck-billed platypus and the country's coat-of-arms. Although colourfully decorated, the central sepia portrait of the Queen is not very high quality and has been poorly cut out which reduces its value significantly.**

£40

▼ Numerous items were made to commemorate the opening of the St Lawrence Sea Way in Canada in 1956 by Queen Elizabeth II. This plate is one of several pieces made by Alfred Meakin bearing an identical print; other examples include a pottery dish. The sepia photographic portraits of the Queen and Duke of Edinburgh are

accompanied by that of Eisenhower, President of the United States at the time, who was also present at the opening. The decoration incorporates a print of the *Royal Yacht Britannia*, together with a map of the Great Lakes. Other items made for the visit include cups and saucers made by Paragon, printed with sepia portraits of the Queen and Prince Philip.

£40

▼ The Queen is held in such high esteem in Britain that visits made by her within the country are still seen as events worth commemorating, par-

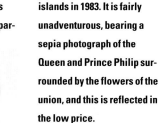

ticularly by the numerous entrepreneurial potters. This mug was produced by John Buck to mark the Queen's opening of the hospital in Chichester in 1985, when she also visited Chichester town hall and Essex University.

£40

▲ This plate made by Weatherby in Stoke-on-Trent commemorates the Queen's visit to the Cayman islands in 1983. It is fairly unadventurous, bearing a sepia photograph of the Queen and Prince Philip surrounded by the flowers of the union, and this is reflected in the low price.

£30

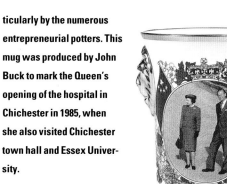

▼ Panorama made this black and white transfer-printed mug for the Queen's visit to the United Sates in her bicentennial year. Mugs of the same shape were made for her visit to West Germany in 1978.

£25

▼ Among the finer pieces marking the Queen's visits is this bone china mug made in a limited edition of 250 by Sutherland exclusively for the Peter Jones Collection in Wakefield, England. The shape and design of the mug is identical to others made for the Queen's 40th Wedding Anniversary by Caverswall. Made for the Queen's first State Visit to China in 1986, it bears an informal picture of the Queen and Duke standing on the Great Wall, which almost looks like a holiday snapshot.

£40

The Thatcher Years

When Margaret Thatcher was elected Conservative Prime Minister on 3 May 1979 she became the first woman Prime Minister in Britain. Under the previous, Labour, government Britain was having a difficult time – relationships between the government and the TUC (Trade Union Congress) had broken down and strikes were widespread throughout the country. Margaret Thatcher introduced a mood of optimism. She was a no-nonsense fighter who took the great Statesman Winston Churchill as her model. She was unmoving in her belief in the privatization of the country's major services. She gained many victories, perhaps the most significant being the Falklands War in 1982/3. Calling a general election shortly after, she won the most decisive victory for 40 years. She also established good relations with the United States, building up a special relationship with the country's president, Ronald Reagan. Her iron resolve earned her the title of the "Iron Lady", a name which she was proud to accept.

The events of the Thatcher years have been well-publicized – television cameras were allowed into the House of Commons for the first time in 1992, and now all government speeches in the Commons are recorded. Numerous commemoratives have been produced of Margaret Thatcher's government. Caricatures of the politicians are particularly popular, especially those created by Fluck and Law.

▲ This mug was produced to commemorate Thatcher's second election victory after the Falklands War in June 1983. It is printed in conservative blue and shows views of the House of Commons and Parliament. The lion is a symbol of British power. On the back is printed the election results – a resounding victory for Margaret Thatcher, showing her popularity with the British public at that time.

£25-35

▼ Margaret Thatcher is seated on a chair bearing the dove of peace. This Toby jug was made to celebrate her 10th anniversary as Prime Minister, and her three raised fingers represent her three election victories. The handbag at her feet has become as much a part of her image as Winston Churchill's cigar was a part of his. This piece has been hand made and hand painted by Kevin Frances Ceramics in Staffordshire, and was modelled by Doug Tootle. It is number 580 in a limited edition of 1,000, which adds to its value.

£100-150

► Few political figures have escaped the cruel treatment of Fluck and Law. Their style is very distinctive and their personalities are instantly recognizable. Although their wares are reasonably affordable today, they will increase in value as Fluck and Law move on to other characters. Pieces depicting Ronald Reagan fetch the highest prices, followed by those of Margaret Thatcher. Other figures in the series include the Queen, Prince Charles, Lady Diana, Prince Andrew and Sarah Ferguson.

£40-60 each teapot

▼ **Margaret Thatcher** served the longest term in office for a prime minister, finally being taken over by John Major in November 1990. This fine quality florit (floral-shaped) dish in deep Tory blue and gilt was made to mark her years in government. It bears a very regal-looking portrait of the Prime Minister, capturing her typical demeanour.

£30-50

▲ ▲ **Dennis Thatcher** appears on few commemoratives. The mug and loving cup are both simple designs and are more utilitarian than decorative. The mug was made for Margaret Thatcher's election victory in 1979, and the loving cup was produced for her resignation in November 1990, in a limited edition of 250.

£25-35 mug

£30-40 loving cup

The Marriage of Prince Andrew and Sarah Ferguson (1836)

The wedding between Prince Andrew and Sarah Ferguson took place on 23 July 1986 at Westminster Abbey. It was a far more restrained affair than the marriage of the first in line to the throne, Prince Charles, to Diana Spencer five years earlier and fewer items were made to mark the event. However, the range is equally diverse, from inexpensive tea towels, playing cards, lapel badges and printed ephemera (even paper plates) to the more expensive and durable cabinet pieces of loving cups, plates and mugs. Ceramics are most popular today, and as with most royal and political figures in the later 20th century, the couple have been the subject of a number of unkind caricatures. Unfortunately the marriage has followed the way of Charles and Diana and their divorce is imminent.

▶ Among the less expensive wares produced for the wedding were biscuit tins bearing the photographs of the happy couple. This example is a fairly uninteresting design, printed in claret and blue, but because such items are quite rare it has become an interesting collectors item, with a relatively high value. Tins with their original contents are even more desirable. **£30-40**

▲ This hand-painted mug is a typical example of the kind of less expensive mass-produced items that were produced for the wedding. The design is original and distinctly modern, but the value is reduced because the mug has not been hand-potted, but mass-produced.

£20-30

▼ One of the best pieces produced to celebrate the marriage is this bone china figurine of Sarah made in a limited edition by Doulton and now withdrawn from production. Although the figure has been slipcast and made in a mould, the finer details, such as the delicate flowers, would have been produced by hand. Unfortunately, the glazing has dulled some of the definition. Although highly collectable, these Doulton figurines are not the finest representations of the royal family, and they tend to be somewhat stilted.

£150-250

▼ Profile portraits became popular during the reign of Victoria and have been used to decorate ceramics ever since. These two mugs hark back to the Victorian age both in their traditional shape and in the "Old English" style of the decoration. The example at the top and bottom was commissioned by the firm of Britannia in London and was made in a limited edition of 150, of which this is number 76. This increases its value to £30-50, whereas the middle one is worth £20-25.

◀ The colour photograph portrait of Sarah Ferguson and Prince Andrew on this bone china plate is one of the most popular images used to decorate the couple's wedding commemoratives. The plate was made by Coalport, who used a similar combination of photographic portrait and decorative floral border to illustrate wares for other royal events.

£20-30

▼ The good quality design on this mug by Richard Guyatt for Wedgwood depicts a profile of the Duke of York as a naval commander; the nautical theme is further emphasized by the waves and the ropes used to weave the Duke's name. The printed decoration is highlighted in gilt. The base bears all the details of the mug, and states the piece is number 935 of 1,000 made.

£80-120

▲ Commemoratives have incorporated processions in their decoration since the early 19th century. This Coalport bone china mug is Victorian in shape and the printed design includes the household cavalry and various equestrian and royal carriages, with Andrew's crown in the centre. It is almost identical to one made by Coalport for Elizabeth's Silver Jubilee, but with a slightly less busy design (see p. 150).

The Queen Mother

The Queen Mother has been loved by the public since she became Queen to George VI in 1937. She particularly gained the affections of the public during the Second World War when she went among the people visiting the injured and the homeless, and despite threats to her personal safety stayed in London alongside her husband, rather than going to North America as the politicians advised. She always maintained a special relationship with her daughter, Elizabeth II, giving her strong support, and helping her take on her life-long role as Queen. She has a passionate interest in horse racing, is very sociable and has established herself as a figurehead and one of the most "human" members of the monarchy. Even in her 90s she still manages to maintain a full weekly diary of events, which she always attends displaying exemplary composure and her warm smile. The majority of commemorative wares have been made for the Queen Mother's later years, particularly for her birthdays, of 75, 80 and 90. Although there are many decorative cabinet wares, such as plates, mugs and figurines, less expensive functional pieces were also made in quantity to appeal to the mass market. Those pieces made by the better makers tend to bear the most satisfying designs. Figurines are particularly collectable, as are commemorative mugs made by British potters.

◀ The colour photograph on this plate made to commemorate the Queen Mother's 80th birthday in 1980 is far more formal than that on the plate on the opposite page, and was taken by Dorothy Wilding. Photographs by Cecil Beaton are particularly desirable and increase the value of a piece considerably. The border is decorated with sepia printed British flora. **£40-50**

▼ Some artistic licence has been taken in the modelling of this Royal Doulton figure made for the Queen Mother's 90th birthday, as she looks far younger than her age. However, the artist Derek Griffiths has managed to capture her regal bearing and serene and pleasant manner and shows her giving her famous smile. The flowers, formal garb and the way she is carrying her handbag are all associated with Elizabeth. This piece was made in a limited edition of 2,500, of which this is number 6, the first in the series to be offered for public subscription and donated by Doulton for auction with the proceeds going to charity. **£250-300**

▲ These mugs commemorating the Queen Mother's 80th and 90th birthdays provide a good selection of the designs produced, and show the varied quality. Those commissioned by the National Trust, of which the Queen Mother was President, are particularly desirable, and are simply decorated with British flora. Like many of the mugs, they were retailed at various stately homes throughout the country owned by the Trust. Apart from the mug bearing the names of the Royal Ladies of August (relating to their birthdays), which is an unusual fluted shape, most are of a fairly basic design, although there are some differences in the handles. **£15-30**

► The black and white photographic print in the centre of this bone china plate is particularly attractive and shows the Queen Mother smiling and wearing a feathered hat. Made for the Queen Mother's 75th birthday in 1975, it was the first of her birthdays to be commemorated. It was made by Panorama Studios in Ashburton. **£30-40**

▼ Very few disposable commemoratives survive and any found, particularly if they are in pristine condi-

◄ The portrait artist Frank Salisbury drew this pastel charcoal portrait of the Queen Mother in 1935, when she was Duchess of York, two years before the coronation of her husband George VI. It is a very good likeness, and illustrates well the type of dress worn at the time. **£1,000-12,000**

tion, are collectable today. Matchboxes have a dual appeal to collectors of memorabilia and to collectors of matchboxes. They should retain their original contents. This example bears an elaborate Victorian design and was made to celebrate the Queen Mother's 75th birthday. **£3-4**

Royal Grandchildren

Surprisingly few commemoratives have been produced for royal births. The first of the Queen's grandchildren was Princess Anne's son, Master Peter Phillips, who was born in 1977. There are only three known types of birth commemoratives for him, and apparently only one, made by Panorama, for his sister, Zara, born in 1981. It was not until the birth of the successor to the throne, Prince William, that birth commemoratives really came to the fore; and the subsequent births of Prince Henry to Charles and Diana, and of Beatrice and Eugenie to Sarah and Andrew have all been more widely celebrated, although such pieces are still relatively rare. Probably the most innovative wares are those using colour photographic images – the process of applying colour photographic images to ceramics had much improved since the time of the Queen's Jubilee in 1977. However, the majority of wares are of debatable artistic merit, and only a few pieces were made by the top makers. Very few, if any, bear portraits of the infants without their parents.

▲ Richard Guyatt designed a range of mugs for Wedgwood to mark the births of Princes Henry and William and Princess Beatrice which are very similar in design. This example for Prince Henry was made in a limited edition of 1,000. It has an unfussy design in royal blue and a silver lustre trim to the handle and rim. Other examples for William are printed entirely in gold and bear the Welsh dragon to symbolize the young Prince's title of Prince of Wales. The mugs were made in a variety of sizes, from small to pint-sized.

£80-100

▶ This is possibly the only type of loving cup produced to mark the birth of Prince William. Made in porcelain by Crown Staffordshire it shows a happy relaxed picture of the parents surrounded by cupids and the Prince of Wales feathers. Beakers exist bearing the same print, with the addition of a small pink crib in the decoration.

£40-50

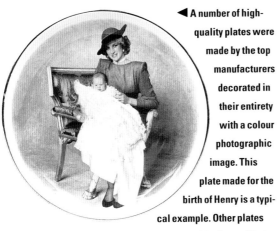

◀ A number of high-quality plates were made by the top manufacturers decorated in their entirety with a colour photographic image. This plate made for the birth of Henry is a typical example. Other plates exist made by Pall Mall with a photograph of the Queen Mother sitting in an identical chair holding the baby.

£30-50

▶ William Dorincourt made this bone china mug for William's birth. The simple design incorporates the Welsh dragon and the English unicorn.

£25-35

▼ John May commissioned this mug to mark the birth of Prince William. The print of the Victorian pram is endearing although rather unusual on a modern-day piece as it is very unlikely to have been used to transport the young Prince through the park. The piece is made even more appealing by the addition of the discarded teddy bear on the ground. **£50-70**

▼ This plate commemorating the birth of Henry was made in a limited edition of 500 by Caverswall, who used the same decorative scroll border on its mugs and beakers. The printing is of good quality and the happy relaxed picture (also found on beakers by the same maker) make it a particularly attractive piece.

£40-60

◀ This beaker marking the birth of Princess Beatrice on 8 August 1988 was made by Caverswall in a limited edition of 250. It is identical in shape and design to a number of other royal commemoratives at this time both by Caverswall, and by Sutherland who produced a beaker to mark the Queen's visit to China (see p. 157). On the reverse are gilt profile portraits of the Duke and Duchess of York.

£35-45

The Queen's 40th Anniversary
(1992)

The 40th anniversary of the Queen's ascension to the throne was celebrated in 1992 and provided yet another opportunity for potters in particular to produce a range of commemoratives. An exhibition was held at the Victoria and Albert Museum in London to coincide with the event and a number of retailers were invited to exhibit their wares there for sale. The exhibition catalogue has since become collectable in its own right. Unfortunately, most of the pottery commemoratives are unadventurous repetitions of designs produced for earlier royal events, and very few show any innovations at all. The most collectable items are those made in limited editions by the top makers.

▼ This loving cup and large plate are part of a series of wares produced by Royal Crown Duchy in Stoke-on-Trent to commemorate the Queen's 40th anniversary and sold at the Victoria and Albert Exhibition in 1992. The print of the Queen is attractive and the design and gilding are of high quality. The portcullis surmounted by the crown on the border of the plate and on the inside of the cup was the official motif adopted by the Anniversary Trust. Made in unlimited quantities these items are relatively inexpensive today.

£15 cup, £30 plate

◄ The fine quality gilding and decoration on this Caverswall plate and the fact that it was made in a limited edition of only 500 make it a very collectable item, worth around £85.

▲ This loving cup was commissioned by the Royal Anniversary Trust for the Queen's anniversary, and bears an unusual design of a crown made up of coloured ribbons. Inexpensive and made in vast quantities, it would have been sold at the Victoria and Albert Museum, as well as through a number of other retail outlets throughout the country. On the base of the cup is the name of the maker – Argyle China Company – and an explaination that it was made under licence for the Trust. Badges were also made bearing the same emblem and these provide a very inexpensive area for the collector of commemoratives.

£12 cup, £2 badge

HER MAJESTY
THE QUEEN'S
40TH ANNIVERSARY

◀ Most of the potters worked with the same official photograph of the Queen to adorn their wares, but used it in different ways. The design on this mug and plate made by the minor firm of Springdale in Stoke-on-Trent is much less successful than that on the pieces by Caverswall. The basket-weave border on the plate is interwoven with miscellaneous flowers, suggesting that a blank has been haphazardly transfer printed, to suggest it was specifically made as a royal commemorative; the border more often bears the flowers of union. **£8-10 each**

▼ Caverswall made a number of commemoratives for the Queen's 40th anniversary using the same design, but in different variations. The 9in (22.5cm) plate on the right was made in a limited edition of 1,000, and although not as attractive as the one on the previous page, is still of fine quality. The same design has been applied to the mug on the left, which was also produced by Caverswall. Both have been attractively highlighted in gilt.

£20 each

Royal Divorces

A new and rather unfortunate collecting area has been created by the many unhappy marriages within the royal family – all three of the seemingly happy marriages of the Queen's children have ended in separation. Any item made to commemorate these events, no matter how poor quality, is highly collectable as such pieces are very rare. The once-private lives of the royal family have in recent years become public knowledge as the press has flouted all measures of decency to delve into the most private lives of the Queen's children.

Andrew Morton's book , *Diana, Her True Story*, caused an uproar when it was published in 1992, as it revealed Diana's most inner life, and it reached even wider audiences when excerpts were printed in all the tabloids. Further scandals ensued with the publishing of tapes recording private telephone calls between Prince Charles and his supposed lover; similarly, pictures have been published of Sarah Ferguson with the American businessman, John Bryant, together with articles romantically linking the couple. These events, along with a recession in Britain and mounting unemployment, led the Queen to call 1992 her "annus horribilis", the only bit of happiness being Princess Anne's remarriage, to Commander Tim Lawrence.

▼ When Queen Elizabeth coined the phrase "annus horibilis" in her Christmas speech it provided the perfect opportunity for pottery manufacturers to produce more commemoratives. The particularly enigmatic smile of the Queen featured on this mug, produced by J. S. Crown of Hale in Cornwall, add to the poignancy of her words.

£30-40

◄ Following on from the divorce of Princess Margaret and Lord Snowdon, was that of Princess Anne and Mark Phillips in 1992. This bone china mug has a portrait of the couple on one side and is decorated on the reverse with a copy of Princess Anne's signed statement. Although the piece is not particularly high quality its rarity means it will increase in value.

£25-35

▼ Items recording the divorce of Princess Margaret and Lord Snowdon on 10 May 1978 are very rare as once the first few were issued further production was stopped by the authorities. It was the first time a royal divorce had been recorded on ceramics – a signal of the liberalization of the British public.

£30-40

Glossary

Amen glass A rare type of Jacobite glass that incorporates into the decoration verses of a Jacobite hymn ending with the word "Amen", thought to date after the Battle of Culloden in 1746. See p. 21.

Anthemion A stylized classical design based on the honeysuckle flower, often featured on wood panelling, oak furniture and plaster friezes.

Appliqué Applied ornamentation which is made separately and then attached to the object. Particularly used on silverwork, pottery and needlework.

Basalt A type of pottery developed c.1767 by Josiah Wedgwood and Thomas Bentley. A hard, black, unglazed, dry body, often painted in red or white in the Greek style and used for Wedgwood's range of Etruscan vases. Also suited to busts, portrait medallions and intaglios.

Beading Moulding in the form of beads used to decorate glass.

Bisque French term for biscuit ware or unglazed porcelain that has only been fired once. Biscuit ware often refers particularly to white porcelain figures which are left undecorated and unglazed.

Black-glazed wares Reddish brown earthenware coated at the biscuit stage with a cobalt pigment and fired at high temperatures which turn the surface almost black. Otherwise known as jetware.

Blue dash chargers Tinglazed earthenware chargers the deep rounded rims of which are decorated with broad dashes of cobalt blue applied with a sponge to suggest twisted rope, copied from the Dutch by Bristol decorators.

Capodimonte A factory in Naples (1743-59) that gave its name to some of the finest porcelain of the 18th century. Moved to Spain 1759 where it continued to produce "Capodimonte" wares.

Caudle cup A silver cup with a cover designed to keep its contents warm. Originally held caudle, a spiced gruel laced with wine.

Cartouche An ornate tablet or shield surrounded by scrollwork and foliage, often bearing an inscription, maker's mark or coat-of-arms.

Castleford wares Porcellaneous white stonewares with relief decoration, usually with blue enamel borders, developed by David Dunderdale of Castleford near Leeds, England from c.1800-1920. Mainly used for jugs and teapots. When held up to the light they look semi-translucent.

Celluloid Developed in the 1870s as a lightweight alternative to bisque, used to produce dolls as well as a vast range of household goods.

Charger A large flat plate or dish often in delftware or slipware popular for commemoratives from c.1630 to the middle of the 18th century.

Chinoiserie Chinese-style decoration featuring Chinese landscapes, birds, figures, fences and dragons, applied to glass, silver and ceramics, and particularly popular during the late 18th century.

Composition dolls Dolls made of an inexpensive substance composed of, variously, cloth, size, wood, wood pulp, plaster of Paris, glue and sawdust.

Creamware First developed by Josiah Wedgwood in the early 1760s. A combination of cream-coloured earthenware and a butter-coloured opaque glaze made to imitate porcelain. It became so popular that it soon became the staple of many potteries.

Cricketania Collecting of items associated with cricket.

Delftware (Dutch) Tin-glazed pottery produced initially in Antwerp from 1512. By the early 17th century Delft was a key area of production and soon its name was applied to all English and Dutch wares of this type. Initially showed a Chinese influence, but in the 18th century also influenced by Europe.

Delftware Tin-glazed earthenware made in England from c.1550. Initially known as "galleyware", it became known as delftware in the Georgian times. It is distinguished from Dutch Delftware by the English use of a small letter "d".

Die-casting Items made from metal or plastic formed under pressure in a mould. Techniques used by Meccano, in Britain, and Dowst under the trade name of Tootsie Toys, in Chicago, for a range of toys.

Dry bodied stoneware Fine textured stoneware, non-porous and unglazed, sometimes with the translucence of porcelain. Production dominated by Wedgwood.

Etruscan ware Stoneware imitation of red-figure ancient Roman pottery made in Tuscany between the 8th and 4th centuries BC which was strongly influenced by ancient Greek models.

Faïence Name taken from the Italian town of Faenze, but used to describe tin-glazed earthenwares (known as maiolica in Italy) made in France, Germany and Scandinavia.

Finial An ornamental apex, particularly on the cover of a tureen or similar, where it serves as a handle. In silver spoons, the ornamanted piece at the opposite end of the shaft to the bowl.

Flatback Brightly-coloured Staffordshire figures with flat undecorated backs made for mantelpieces

Flo(w) An underglaze blue decoration with blurred lines which was originally a fault, but which is now sought after by collectors.

Florit Floral shaped glass and silverware.

Footrim The shaped rim under plates, dishes, saucers, and on hollow wares.

Gin flask A stoneware jar or flask, in the 19th century often modelled as a caricature of a political or royal figure.

Gimmel A double flask with spouts facing in opposite directions, usually of clear or lightly tinted transparent glass.

Honiton lace A fine bobbin lace whose designs consist mainly of naturalistic sprays, mostly floral, although shells and butterflies also feature. The best examples include raised elements worked in by sewing in threads into the existing pinholes.

Intaglio Incised decoration, the opposite of carving in relief.

Intarsia ware Inlaid pieces of different coloured woods used to form a picture.

Jacobite glass Wine glasses engraved with symbols of the Jacobites, made from 1746 to 1788.

Jasperware Fine-grained white vitrified stoneware with translucent properties developed by Josiah Wedgwood c.1776. Usually coloured to make "solid jasper", but after 1780 objects were often dipped into a vessel of coloured jasper slip. Wedgwood blue is one of the best known examples. Decoration is usually applied in white relief.

Jetware See black-glazed wares.

Lineralia Items associated with famous liners (i.e. *The Titanic*, see p. 101).

Lithophane A translucent panel of biscuit porcelain with intaglio moulded decoration incorporated into a porcelain body. Frequently used to depict portraits, figural groups and landscapes.

Lobed A rounded projection forming part of a larger structure.

Maiolica 16th-century Italian earthenwares moulded in high relief and decorated with enamels in a palette of ochres, browns, whites, turquoises, pinks and greens. Reproduced in the Victorian period by such potteries as Mintons.

Marquetry The design formed from different coloured woods veneered onto a carcass to give a decorative effect.

Mezzotint A print made from engraved copper or steel plates treated so as to achieve subtle tonal gradations.

Naive Primitive artistic style.

Onglaze High temperature colours applied to ceramics over the glaze.

Parian A type of porcelain with a matt, semi-translucent, ivory-coloured body which resembles marble,

developed as a substitute for the white biscuit figures popularized by Sèvres and others in the 18th and early 19th century.

Pearlware A type of pottery developed by Josiah Wedgwood as a whiter-bodied alternative to the firm's successful creamwares. Ideal for transfer printing.

Queensware The alternative name given by Wedgwood to its creamwares in honour of Queen Charlotte who specially commissioned a dinner service from Wedgwood in 1767. Copied and used by many others.

Prattware Light-coloured or buff clay earthenware decorated with a limited range of high temperature colours of yellow, blue, brown and green, popularized by Felix Pratt, but widely produced in the late 18th and 19th centuries. Particularly used for jugs moulded in relief with borders of stylized foliage, depicting famous personalities, such as Nelson (see pp. 40-41).

Ribbon plates Plates with holes in the border through which to thread ribbons for hanging on a wall.

Rococo A style associated with Louis XV (1715-74) which came to England in the mid-18th century.

Rococo porcelain is associated with the Sèvres factory in France. The style is characterized by asymmetric curvaceous shapes and soft, feminine colours such as pink and yellow. Scrolls are a key feature – for example on the bases of figures – and shells, rocks, floral and leaf motifs were also favoured.

Saltglaze A glazed stoneware. Salt is added to the kiln during firing to created a glaze pitted like an orange skin. White saltglaze can resemble porcelain. Buff, red and brown types were used for utilitarian objects.

Slip A creamy mixture of clay and water used to decorate pottery.

Slipware English reddish brown or buff earthenware decorated largely with a coating of slip which sometimes was scraped and cut away to make patterns, showing the underneath colour of earthenware. Zig-zag, feathered and marble designs predominate. The body was then covered in a lead-based glaze which gave a streaky yellow colour to the piece.

Spelter Zinc alloyed with lead used in the 19th century to produce inexpensive decorative cast articles such as candlesticks and clock cases.

Spelter disease Damage to spelter items when the underneath alloy can be seen through the lead.

Sponging On ceramics, the application of colours over a thick glaze with the use of a sponge, particularly popular with the Staffordshire potters. Also known as spatterware.

Stevengraph A silk picture made on a modified form of the Jacquard weaving machine by Thomas Stevens of Coventry, but later applied to those made by other makers.

Stippling A method of engraving which involved tapping and scratching a glass surface with a diamond point to create a pattern of minute dots and dashes.

Stumpwork Particularly popular during the reign of Charles II. Panels of needlework with distinctive areas of raised decoration formed by padding details in the design or covering areas of wood with silk or satin. Such areas often applied with tiny seed pearls and sequins. Used to decorate small caskets and as frames for mirrors.

Tazza A wide but shallow bowl on a stem with a foot in ceramic, metal or glass.

Tin glaze An opaque white glaze of tin oxide, characteristic of Delftware (Holland), faïence (Germany) and maiolica (France).

Trivet A metal three-legged stand placed in front of a fire for cooking implements to be placed on.

Tyg A three-handle drinking cup.

Underglaze Decoration, usually painted or printed, applied before glazing.

Cobalt blue is the most popular colour.

Wemyss ware Hand-painted pottery produced by Thomas Goode & Co.'s factory in Fife, Scotland, decorated in a distinctive palette of greens, pinks, browns and purples, with motifs of brightly painted and realistic fruits, flowers, animals, birds and insects.

Bibliography

Clarke, John *George III*, Weidenfeld & Nicholson, 1972
The Collector's Encyclopedia, Victoriana to Art Deco, Studio Editions, 1990
Collins Encyclopedia of Antiques, Tiger, 1973
Davey, M. H. & Mannnion, D. J. *Fifty Years of Royal Commemorative China 1887-1937*, Dayman Pubs, 1988
Davey, M. H. & Mannion, D. J. *Four Generations of Royal Commemorative China 1936-1990*, Dayman Pubs, 1991
Feild, Rachael *Buying Antique Pottery and Porcelain*, Macdonald, 1987
Hibbert, Christopher *The Story of England*, Phaidon, 1992
Hughes, Thurle *The Country Life Antiques Handbook*, Country Life, 1986
Longford, Elizabeth *The Oxford Book of Royal Anecdotes*, OUP, 1989
Marshall, Dorothy *The Life and Times of Victoria*, Weidenfeld & Nicholson, 1972
Osborne, Harold, ed *The Oxford Companion to the Decorative Arts*, OUP, 1975
Palmer, Alan *The Penguin Dictionary of Modern History 1789-1945*, Second Edition, Penguin, 1983
Priestley, J. B. *The Prince of Pleasure and his Regency*, Heinemann, 1969
Savage, G. *Dictionary of Antiques*, Barrie and Jenkins, 1970
Williams, E. N. *The Penguin Dictionary of English and European History 1485-1789*, Penguin, 1980
Williamson, David *Kings and Queens of Britain*, Webb & Bower, 1992

Index

Acknowledgments

The publishers would like to thank the following auction houses,
museums, dealers, collectors and other sources for supplying pictures for use in this book
or for allowing their pieces to be photographed.

14SL, 15B, 16tlB, trP, bSL; 17tlB, trCL, blSL, brSL; 18tB, bCNY; 19tSL, blCS, brB; 20tlCS, cCS, blCS, brCS; 21tSL, cSL, bCS; 22tCS, 23SL, 24tB, bB; 25tB, clB, crSL, blSL, brSL; 26tSL, cB, bB; 27tSL, trCS, blCL, brSL; 30tB, bSL; 31tlB, trSL, cB, blB, brSL; 32tB, bCL; 33tB, cCNY, bSL; 34B; 35RD; 36tB, cB, bB; 37tB, cB, bH&G; 38tJM, cJM, bJM; 39tJM, cJM, blB; 40tJM, bB; 41tJM, cJM, blJM, brMB; 42tJM, bB; 43tlJM, trCL, blJM, brJM; 44tBr, cBr, bJM; 45tlBr, trJM, blBr, brB; 46tSL, bH&G; 47tlJM, trH&G, blJM, brBr; 48lBr, rJM; 49tH&G, clJM, crJM, bJM; 50JM; 51SL; 52tBr, cB, rB;53tH&G, cH&G, bB;tB, bB; 55tlB, trSL, crJM, bJM; 56tB, bH&G; 57tlB, trH&G, cB, blH&G, brB; 58tH&G, 59H&G, 60tB, cJM, bB; 61tB,clB, crB, blH&G, brJM; 62tB, bB; 63tlB, trB, blH&G, brJM; 64B; 65RD; 66blMB, rB, 67B; 68tH&G, bB; 69tlB, trB; blB, brCSK; 70tH&G, cH&G, bBr; 71tlH&G, trH&G, clB, crB, blMB, brH&G; 72tBr, cBr, bH&G; 73tB, cP, bP; 74tB, blB, brJM; 75tH&G, bH&G; 77tlH&G, trH&G, cH&G, bH&H; 78tH&G, cH&G, bH&G; 79tBr, cBr, lBr; 80tJM, cB, bMB, 81tH&G, cblB, brH&G; 82tB, lBr; 83tlB, trBr, blBr, brH&G; 84tH&G, bH&G; 85tlH&G, trH&G, cBr, blH&G, brBr; 86tH&G, cBr, bBr; 87tBr, clJM, crB, bBr; 88tBr, H&G; 89tlSF/MB, clBr, cH&G, blBr, brH&G; 90JM; 91JM; 92tH&G, cH&G, bH&G; 93trH&G, clH&G, crH&G, bG&G; 94tBr, blH&G, brBr; 95tH&G, cH&G, brB; 96SL; 97RD; 98tlB, cH&G, bH&G; 99tMB, cH&G, rH&G; 100tB, cMB, blB, brB; 101tB, bCSK; 102tBr, crH&G, clH&G, bBr; 103tJM, cH&G, blH&G, brH&G; 104tH&G, cBr, bH&G; 105tlH&G, trH&G, cBr, bH&G; 106tlBr, cBr, bCSK; 107tlBr, trBr, blBr, brB; 108tH&G, bBr; 109tlH&G, trBr, cB, blH&G, brH&G; 110tH&G, bH&G, 111tlH&G, trH&G, blH&G, brSP; 112tH&G, cBr, Br; 113tlH&G, trBr, bBr; 114tJM; 115B; 116tH&G, cH&G, bH&G; 117tlH&G, trBr, cH&G, bH&G; 118tH&G, bH&G; 119tH&G, cB, bMB; 120JM; 121JM; 122tH&G, cB, bH&G; 123tBr, cH&G, blMB, brH&G; 124tB, c&bB; 125tB, clH&G, crBr, blB, brH&G; 126tB, cBr, bBr; 127tBr, cBr, bBr; 128tBR, bBr; 129t&blBr, tcMB, trBr, cB, brBr; 130tH&G, bH&G; 131Br(all); 132tBr, bBr; 133tBr, cH&G, bB; 134JM; 135JM; 136tB, cB, bH&G; 137tlH&G; trH&G, cH&G, blH&G, brB; 138tH&G, blJG, brMB; 139tB, cH&G, blB, brMB; 140tH&G, bH&G; 141tH&G, clBr, crBr, bBr; 142tBr, cH&G, bH&G; 143trBr, clJM, crJM, blJM, brBr; 144tBr, cBR, bH&G; 145tl H&G, trH&G, cH&G, blBr, brJM; 146tBr, cBr, bH&G; 147tlB, trBr, blH&G, crBr; 148tB, bB; 149tMB; cH&G, bH&G; 150tlH&G, trB, cJM, blMB; 151tBr, trH&G, clJM, Br; 152tB, bH&G, 153tMB, crH&G, blB; 154tCL, clMB, bcB, brH&G; 155tH&G, cCSK, blB, brRD; 156tH&G, cJM, bBr; 157tH&G, clH&G, crBR, blBr, brMB; 158tBr, bH&G, 159tlBrm, H&G, trBr, blBr; 160tlBr, cRD, bMB, 162tH&G, bB; 163tlMB, trH&G, cMB, bMB; 164tH&G, bH&G, 165tlH&G, trH&G, cBR, blBr, brBr; 166lH&G, rH&G; 167tlH&G, trH&G, bH&G; 168tBR, cBR, bBR

Key

b bottom, c centre, r right

B	Bonham's, London	MB	Mitchell Beazley
Br	Britannia, Grays Antique Market, London	P	Phillip's London
CL	Christie's, London	RD	Richard Dennis, Ilminster
CNY	Christie's New York	SL	Sotheby's, London
CS	Christie's, Scotland	SNY	Sotheby's, New York
CSK	Christie's, South Kensington	SP	Sue Pearson
H&G	Hope and Glory, London	SF/MB	Stephen Furniss, Asters Antiques, Shene, Surrey
JM	John May, J&J May, London		

176